THE
INVISIBLE
HAND

BOGDAN J. WNUK

Palmetto Publishing Group
Charleston, SC

The Invisible Hand
Copyright © 2020 by Bogdan J. Wnuk

All rights reserved No portion of this book may be reproduced, stored in a retrieval system, or transmitted in any form by any means–electronic, mechanical, photocopy, recording, or other–except for brief quotations in printed reviews, without prior permission of the author.

First Edition

Printed in the United States

ISBN-13 978-1-64111-756-2
ISBN-10: 1-64111-756-7

DEDICATION

This book is dedicated to my wife and my son, who, by taking "abuse" positively, turned their respective past miseries into bright futures.

CONTENTS

Part I ···1

Chapter 1   Why me, why France? ························ ·3
Chapter 2   Puppy love and silent movie ················ 11
Chapter 3   Mister the Priest (Monsieur le Cure) ······· 22
Chapter 4   "Michelin" and the American cartoons ······· 31
Chapter 5   The traveling "Apatride" ··················· 38
Chapter 6   On the way to Clermont-Ferrand ············· 46
Chapter 7   Anne-Marie ································· 57
Chapter 8   Meeting my girl ···························· 64
Chapter 9   From Helios to Heliopolis ·················· 75

Part II ··89

Chapter 10   A ticket to America ······················· 91
Chapter 11   The Invisible Hand ·······················103
Chapter 12   When Melancholy meets Nostalgia ··········113
Chapter 13   The new: "Normal" ························122
Chapter 14   Retiring from active duty ················135
Chapter 15   The last hurdle ··························144
Chapter 16   Argentina ································154
Chapter 17   At peace, at last (part I): France ·······165
Chapter 18   At peace, at last (part II): America ·····173
Chapter 19   The mystery of faith ·····················183

PART I

CHAPTER 1

WHY ME, WHY FRANCE?

I am writing these lines from my newly acquired house on Singer Island in South Florida. Even three months ago, I had no idea that this place existed, needless to say that I would buy it!

When I consider my life, in retrospect, I find amazing to see myself in places that I have never planned to be at. Usually things in life are planned in advance, but in this case, as in many others, it was not… or if it was, I was not aware of the plan or simply did not pay attention to its unfolding. Actually as I look at the place, which we decided to name: the "Garden of Eden", with its lush tropical vegetation around the swimming pool and the shuffle board court, I recall that, at the young age of ten or eleven, I was fascinated by pictures of the tropics, the tiny islands in the vast oceans, the emerald-blue waters, the coconut trees and, out of my pre adolescent imagination, pretty scantily-clad girls with big boobs and curvy butts sunbathing lasciviously on golden sandy beaches.

Recalling these memories may make my acquisition look like the completion of a dream come true. In fact, even though it would be tempting to make believe that all was pre-planned to make it happen, since the realization of my love for the tropics, it would be far from any truth or actual reality. Hence the question: "what brought me here?" calls for an answer that I will try to fathom with all the resources of my memory and imagination…

For some people, moving from place to place, changing jobs or partners or friends, making love, having kids or dogs or cats, living and dying and then some are just uneventful stages or moments in life which deserve no consideration other than going through the motions, with the flow, seldom questions asked, if any at all, whether these stages and moments were one's own decisions or somebody else's, whether one liked it or not… For me, I believe that every event in life has a meaning, that all events are connected to each other with a sense of purpose and that, from beginning to end, the sense of purpose shapes our lives in unexpected ways through the people who originated them.

As far as I am concerned, the "unexpected" began with War World Two and a certain Mister: "Adolph Hitler" who, in his megalomaniac view of the world, decided to invade Poland, after a couple of successful annexations of independent countries in Europe, cowardly authorized by the infamous "Munich agreement". In Poland, at that time, lived two young people in their mid twenties, my future father and mother. Father was a peasant working in his father's farm nearby the town of "Kalisz". He was a country boy with no schooling and a limited knowledge and understanding of the world around him when, one day, he was removed from his native farm by German soldiers and deported, by train, to a remote place in Germany to work in another farm. The change between his former and his new live was minimal. The major difference was the language. He neither understood nor spoke German… and he missed his family. For my mother, born in "Czestochowa", grown up in "Krakow" and studying in "Warszawa", at that time, it was a different story. As a student at the University she was very much in tune with the events of the time. She followed the rise of Nazism in neighboring Germany and, in her mind, prepared for the worse. When once the Germans debarked in the capital of Poland to round up the opposition to the occupation, she was there, and as so many others, arrested and deported to Germany to work in the industries deserted by male workers called to the front.

Father worked in a farm and mother in a factory. Years passed and finally the day of liberation came. All prisoners subjected to forced labor during the war were regrouped in refugee camps controlled by the "United Nations Organization". It was in one of them, in "Haltern", Germany, that Dad and Mom met, fell in love and got married. Life in the camp was boring and drinking schnapps (a German version of Polish Vodka) was the favorite pastime. The liberated ones had not much to do… but wait for the U.N. administration to clear their way back home or to find a new beginning as immigrants. Dad was tall, handsome and street smart. Mom was a charming petite and an intellectual. How these two fell in love is yet to be figured out, but they did, and that love produced: ME! Needless to say that my birth was not planned by myself, neither were my parents of my own choosing! Nevertheless, there I was. Mother knew that, by the "Yalta accords", the western allies gave Poland to "Stalin". That fact by and in itself was not negotiable as far as returning to, now, Communist Poland. Father was disappointed. For our sake mother applied for immigration to many different countries and the wait for a visa began… Had "Yalta" kept Poland free from communism, I suppose we would have all moved from Germany to Poland without hesitation. Daddy would have been very happy and I would have grown up as a typical "Polack" with a name perfectly fit in the land of "Poles": "Bogdan Wnuk", which, word for word, translates as the "God-given Grandson". For this not to happen, I must thank the trio consisting of: "Roosevelt", "Churchill" and "Stalin" for influencing directly my ultimate move to the United States of America some thirty years later…

After a year or so, a visa was granted. It was a French visa, not the most desired American one or the second on line Canadian, neither the far fetch ones from Australia or New-Zeeland, not even one from Sweden which was the before last choice to France. At that time, the culturally Anglo-Saxon countries were in favor of accepting couples without children, for they were looking for laborers undisturbed by raising kids, or costing them money by paying social security benefits to families in needs with young kids. Unfortunately I was there and my presence greatly determined the visa outcome. When the application for a French visa was approved, without a second thought, my parents set-off to France since waiting hopelessly in lifeless drunken German camps was out of question.

Father left for France, first. He took the train and after a couple of days of travel, ended up in a farm called "Chateau-Gaillard" in the municipality of "Orleat" close to the small town of "Lezoux", nearby the big town of "Clermont-Ferrand", the capital of the "Auvergne" region. Here again, the change for him was minimal. The major difference was the language. My father did not understand nor spoke French. Once father settled down, my mother and I left Haltern in Westphalia, Germany, where I was born.

Now I was in France, needless to say not by my own will… What about that as far as planning my life in the USA? Well, time will tell!

The landlord of Chateau-Gaillard had a family and three kids: two boys and a girl. The youngest one of my age was the closest to me and, at the great age of sixteen months, we were hanging out together most of the days. Very quickly I learned French, a "baby French" mind you, nevertheless it was the beginning of my "career" as a translator to my parents from "baby Polish", which I was learning from them, to "baby French".

My intellectual mother was a fast learner compared to my father: the hillbilly. Soon, she was able to converse with the boss of Chateau-Gaillard. The working visa issued by the French government was binding. My father and mother could not change work for three years, unless they changed their mind and re-applied for an immigration visa to another country during the first year of their stay abroad. During that first year however, my mother became pregnant again and this fact alone distracted my parents from even thinking about moving while they were barely making their marks in their newly adopted country.

My sister: "Christine", was born in the town of "Thiers", a town nearby where we lived, with a hospital, and baptized shortly after in the village of "Saint Jean d'Heur", the closest place to Chateau-Gaillard with a church and a priest. The house we all lived in was small. It was composed of one room in the first floor which was all at once the kitchen, the dining room and the living room. On the second floor was the bedroom with the master bed for my parents and two cribs for my sister and me. The furnishing was used and old but sufficient to accommodate the frugal needs of the family. We were living on the products of the farm. Vegetables from the garden and meats from livestock: mainly chicken and rabbit but also pork and beef grown on the farm for the landlord's family but also for the permanent or occasional farm workers living on site. Shopping for food was unknown to us and shopping for home goods was carried out once a month in the town of "Lezoux" or "Pont du Chateau", by the landlord, chauffeuring himself his wife and my mother in the well kept black "Citroen traction 15".

The first real conversation between my mother and Mr. Coutarel was about pay. Although food was considered as a payment in nature, and it was plentiful, my father and mother were underpaid as far as real money was concerned. Mother was always worrying about me and my sister growing up and the need to send us to school, the desire to emerge from the relative misery the family was in, the dream to become middle-class citizen, own a house, build a white picket fence around the house and the garden and wear our "Sunday best clothes" from morning mass to evening vespers… The conversation did not go well. Very quickly, the landlord realized that my mother did her homework and had together all the facts for winning the argument.

The reason for this to happen was because Chateau-Gaillard was neighboring two other "Chateaux" or big farms. One was named: "Ravel" and the other: "La Rapine". These two Chateaux were also tended by two Polish immigrant families. The three Chateaux were at a one to two hour walking distance of one another and the three families were often together, on Sundays, in turns, at each other places. This is where my mother was getting her news of the world and updates on their situation as immigrants and political refugees. Actually the other families had radios and were listening to news from Poland on a short wave channel called "Volna Polska", ironically meaning: "Free Poland"!

The landlord feared to be reported to the U.N. refugee agency in Clermont-Ferrand and agreed to give her a raise but also learned that my parents were looking for a better paying job and that they will be leaving the farm on the very last day of the three years binding working visa. At this moment, I suppose that he was regretting having put together the three Polish families for humanitarian reasons so that they could speak their language and share their traditions in a foreign environment… Of course the landlord was very disappointed since he knew he would never find any laborers, locally, as cheap as my parents were, specially, almost five years, after the end of World War Two... I was disappointed too. For me, the life at the farm was fascinating! With my little friend "Alain", we were running around in the fields and in the woods. We were also fishing frogs in the large pond were the landlord was raising carps. I will never forget the thrill of trying to grab the big fish which were slipping from our tiny hands when the pond was emptied once a year. I remember also the joyful time of wheat harvesting when all the farmers were joining forces to get the grains from fields to bags. What intrigued me the most was a noisy machine which was fed, on one end, with random wheat cuts and which was delivering bags of grains and bundles of straw at the other end. Most of the noise was due to the squeaking of the pulleys and belts and the roaring of a steam engine. My worst souvenir was at one of these harvesting feasts when the landlord killed a fat calf, for the occasion, in order to feed the workers in attendance. It was my calf... My father who delivered it just about a year or so before - and I attended the whole time of the delivery - told me that it was mine! So I took care of him by visiting him every day, either in the stable or in the field where he was pasturing with other calves and older cows. I liked his big eyes and we could see each other eye to eye since we were of just about the same height. On that harvest day, I saw him hanging from the cross beam of the door of the stable, head down and his back legs set apart and nailed to the beam. My eyes were red for resisting crying but my heart was bleeding...

Everybody seemed to be happy, I was devastated!

I do not remember too well the harvesting of tobacco, which was the main crop of Chateau-Gaillard, but do remember the pleasure my father was having hanging the large leaves on long steel wires running from one end of the barn to the other for the leaves to dry.

My father was happy to be paid in food, wine, "gnole" (which is a French version of Polish vodka or German schnapps) and tobacco leaves. In a back room in our small house, he was tending his share of tobacco leaves as if it was a treasure since he was trading them for booze…

The other memories I took with me when we departed; for one, was a glance on the wheat fields where, one day, my father returning from Ravel, drunk, demolished his bike, by kicking it hard, because the poor thing did not want to ride in mud; for the other, it was the staircase in the house, leading to the bedroom, where my mother was seating often and crying all the tears of her soul over her loneliness and my father's drunkenness; and for last it was the vegetable garden adjacent to our house where once, on a hot summer day, Alain and I fell asleep, drunk, after having emptied a bottle of wine left by my father on the kitchen table…

CHAPTER 2

PUPPY LOVE AND SILENT MOVIE

The pick-up truck of the owner of "Laiterie de Theix", the milk processing plant of the village of "Theix", in the volcanoes mountain chain of the region Auvergne, left Chateau-Gaillard with my mother and baby sister in the cabin of the truck and dad and I in the back open bed with our meager belongings. I was well over 4 years old when we finally stopped in the middle of the village of Theix in the heart of the volcanic mountains bordering the town of Clermont-Ferrand in the south west.

In September of 1951 I attended school for the first time. What an experience it was! We were eighteen pupils of all ages ranging from four to fourteen. The youngest ones were on the left side of the classroom and the oldest on the right. The teacher was tending, at the same time, six different programs. He must have been a magician because I never remember having felt being left alone ever even when he was teaching other children a different program... I loved school and school loved me in return. Very quickly I became the poster child used by my teacher to represent the school at scheduled academic inspections. At each visit, I showed my notebooks to the inspector (each time a different one) and answered questions relative to my level of learning. I was good and I felt good. My mother was very proud of me. My father might have been too, but it did not show…

In December of 1951, to be precise on the 6th of December of 1951, I came across something special. In the evening of that cold and snowy day my parents invited an old man for dinner (at least he looked old to me) wearing a brown robe, open toe sandals and a long grey beard. A rope was wrapped around his robe at the waist with a cross hanging at one end of the rope. I was told he was a traveling Catholic monk on an evangelical Christmas mission in the area. The priest of the parish enlisted most of his parishioners to invite the monk, at least once for one meal, for the whole duration of his mission. On the evening of the 6th of December was my parents' turn. The food was great. Eggs, poultry, pork, potatoes, cheeses and cakes were coming and going seamlessly. The monk was full and ended his meal with a couple of shots of gnole (French moonshine for the American amateurs) to supplement a good liter of red wine he downed during the dinner. At this point, with his face red as a lobster, he leaned back on his chair and began to tell us (the kids) the story of "Saint Nicholas" which is celebrated on the 6th of December in most part of the Saxon and Slavic continental nations of Europe. Saint Nicholas, he insisted, not "Santa Claus"! I knew Saint Nicholas and, at my young age, was thrilled at the idea of getting presents, passed to us, by him, through our parents as a reward to our good deeds. My sister was too young to understand anything of what was happening or what the monk said but was charmed by his loud talking and mainly by his spectacular circumvoluted hand motions which made her burst in occasional laughter that made everybody laugh!

My parents were delighted to hear a French monk speaking so well of one of their tradition, so dear to them, but mainly unknown in France as well as in most other European Latin countries, except for the French regions of "Alsace" and "Lorraine" which were once possessions of Germany. After sharing the gifts, as a symbol to demonstrate our love to one another, the monk went on and talked about someone who was born in "Bethlehem" on the 25th of December, at "Christmas" time, in a manger. His name was "Jesus". According to the monk, Jesus was the gift that God gave us, not only to enjoy life down here, on earth, but also to keep on enjoying life, after death, in Heaven, if we only believed in him. At that time, I did not know that Jesus was a "gift of God" and did not fully understand either the notion of "Heaven" or what "believing in Him" meant… but, for sure, I knew Jesus for the occasion He gives to celebrate, at Christmas, with a good supper meal and plenty of cookies and candies after the meal. In my little head, I figured that, maybe, "the good meal" itself was the gift of "enjoyment" that God wanted us to have to celebrate the birth of Jesus, as His gift to us, which keeps on giving in order to enjoy life down here, on earth, and later in Heaven… as the monk said! I was not sure, nevertheless I knew that, in my family, the Christmas meal was always very enjoyable…

I remember, till this day, that the way the monk talked about Jesus was more spellbinding than the most fascinating fairy tale I have ever heard and I thank, to this day, my parents for having invited that monk on that 6th of December. Although the magic of Saint Nicholas was still working (mainly because of the gifts, I am sure!) I started to obsess about that new mystery person called Jesus.

When came spring of 1952, around Easter time, I began to go to catechism. There I learned everything about the mystery man Jesus, born in Bethlehem, in a manger. I was told that he walked on water, was followed by a crowd of thousands, spoke to the crowds in "parables" (which sounded like fairy tales), changed water into wine (my father certainly liked that), fed huge crowds with two loafs of bread and five fish, gave his sight back to the blind and made the lame walk, resurrected his friend Lazarus, preached love and forgiveness, forgave the sinners, scourged the so-called: righteous and, because of that, endured all the harshest beatings that our evil world had to offer, including death on a cross… and that he survived all of that by resurrecting himself on the third day of his death. What a man! What a powerful man! What a Superman! What a God! I dreamt of becoming like him. He quickly became my hero. What I had some hard time to figure out - and perhaps some others like me - was what his punishment and death had to do with salvation… and why we needed salvation! In order to help us understand, the priest told us a story which once and for good put the issue to rest. The priest said that at one time he discovered that some money from collections was regularly stolen and, overtime, everything led him to believe that one of the altar boys did it. When he assembled the group of seven suspects no one said a world. After a short wait the priest decided that if no one pleads: guilty, all of us will, collectively, be punished, as accomplices, for the theft and that subsequently all perks, including monthly church money allowances, will be suppressed for the following month. Just before disbanding one guy denounced himself as the thief. Nobody could believe it was him… neither the priest who knew who did it. None the less the priest played the game to the end by reinstating the perks to everybody but him. The innocent one, for the love of his team mates, took the blame and the punishment in order to save them…

That is exactly what Jesus did as the innocent "lamb of God" who once and for all took away the sin of the world and, in so doing, reconciled God and His rebellious Creation! The Jewish tradition, at Passover, before, during and after Jesus' time, which consists in slaying a lamb and its blood offering, which is supposed to cover the sins of the Jews, every year and for a year, was and still is a contemporary reminder of Jesus' salvational mission which Christians celebrate at Easter.

What was less appealing about catechism was all the stuff called: commandments of the church, laws and traditions. I understood that some were from God but others were from the government of the Catholic Church, which, according to the priest, represents the "Will of God" on earth… and even some others from the "Fathers" of the church who were the great thinkers and philosophers of ancient and modern times. That stuff was an endless list of do's and don'ts which were supposed to get us to Heaven, where Jesus lives, if we were to follow them "religiously". My notion of getting to Heaven was still the one of the monk who so nicely said that: "Jesus was the gift that God gave us not only to enjoy life down here, on earth, but also to keep on enjoying life, after death, in Heaven, if we only believed in him." And what a believer in Him I became!

I have never truly connected the life of Jesus with the catechism stuff which we all had to memorize, by heart, and recite, word for word, in order to make the grades for the sacrament of the "Solemn Communion". For me, this Holy Sacrament of the Catholic church, was still seven years away but, I knew that my records will follow me, from parish to parish, until that time comes and that all of my good and bad deeds will be evaluated and used to determine my faith and willingness to become a good Catholic.

The teaching of catechism was not in Theix but in a village, three kilometers away, where resided the priest who was in charge of four villages within the same parish. Therefore, once a week, on Thursday mornings, a little troupe of boys and girls was gathering on the central place of the village before beginning the long march through meadows and a wood until reaching the church of "Saint-Genes-Champanelle" where the priest was waiting for us.

Among my friends, one girl: "Monique", grabbed my attention… almost at first glance, on my first day of school and became my: "bonne-amie" that I thought was spelled: "bonami". We would say "girlfriend" in English. I knew that she liked me because she was always next to me to the point that, not only in school, but here also at catechism, the priest, as the teacher, had to separate us in order to avoid distraction. The way catechism was taught was funny. Since we did not have a classroom with desks and chairs the priest had us to seat on the kneeling board of the pews in the church and use the bench as a desk.

So it was! Monique was my "bonami" and the other kids were mocking us by calling us "les (plural) bonamis"! Actually, instead of being offended, I was proud and liked the name calling because, deep in me, it was associated with a feeling of warmth and tenderness towards Monique. I did not know yet what love was about, but I knew that I have never experienced such a feeling, ever, in my life, before. We were holding hands while walking across the fields and the wood which were on our way to the church. One day, we found ourselves separated from the group. The grass was tall and warm. It was mid-Autumn and the leaves were turning to a flamboyant pallet of colors. Without realizing what was happening we were lying on the ground in the tall grass… kissing each other tenderly. Neither movies nor television programs were there to teach us how to kiss. We were just kissing as nature intended when a boy and a girl are in love. At that very moment, I realized, in my heart and guts what "unconditional love" was about and what "dying for someone you love" meant; words I heard in the priest's mouth many times but only when he was speaking of Jesus. At that very moment, with Jesus as my witness, she was my extension and for a while I was no longer me alone but one with her, through her, in her and by her...

Talking about movies, I saw my first cinematographic show in a bar-restaurant when a couple of peddlers stopped by the village and offered to run the show for twenty cents per person for adults and ten for kids. When we entered the restaurant, the tables were stored in a corner of the room and the chairs were all lined up in six rows of seven. There were almost as many children as adults. For most of us, kids and adults alike, the magic was to begin. Since very few, in the countryside, had the opportunity to go see movies in theaters, like in Clermont-Ferrand, the nearest big town in Auvergne being equipped for such spectacles, the upcoming show was a "premiere". After a moment of flickering frames on the silver screen, the pianist started to play and the actors on the screen began their silent performance only punctuated by written interruptions explaining the course of the events. The show lasted thirty minutes. At the end I was speechless, still under the spell of the magic of what we would call today: virtual reality! Finally, all the male adults gathered at the bar and with a glass of wine on hand they commented and debated loudly what technology could do. Yet, in spite of the technological prowess, few believed that this kind of spectacle will ever become as popular as the performing arts in vogue at that time. Whether the cinema will survive as an art or not was the least concern of the wife of the owner of laiterie de Theix, the dairy plant, and the mayor of the village. She was plump, short, always smiling and her hair cut short too, like a man, which was quite unusual for women back then. She knew about movies but, by her own account, never experienced, in person, the formidable impact of the picture on the kids, including her kids: "Jean", her son and "Marie-Claude", her daughter. Since the projection, at the bar-restaurant, she managed to buy a movie projector and a portable screen and to rent whatever movies for kids were available through a movie-club in Clermont-Ferrand. Her objective was to gather all the kids on Thursday afternoons (there was no class on Thursdays) and spend a couple of hours watching: "Charlie Chaplin" or "Laurel and Hardy" not to mention a bunch of black and white "Disney" cartoons while sipping hot chocolate and eating cookies. She was the presenter, the commentator, the entertainer… and I will never forget that. As far as my father was concerned, noticing my enthusiasm after the peddlers' show, he proposed to take me with him to movie theaters in Clermont-Ferrand every time a movie with the comic actor "Fernandel" was at play. The "Don Camillo" series was his favorite. It was featuring a caricature of the political fight of a conservative Catholic priest: "Don Camillo/Fernandel" and a communist mayor (Pepone) to win the villagers over their respective ideologies. I did some translation, on occasion, and never saw my father laughing so hard. The laughter was a good compensation for the effort he put riding his bicycle (some twenty kilometers, round trip) with me on the back seat.

I just passed my seventh birthday when I overheard, for the first time, conversations between my parents about moving again. I did not want to move. I loved my village, my school and my friends and above all my sweetheart and soul mate Monique. I did not want to leave her. She and I were even closer friends than me and my sister whom I loved also dearly. To my sister, three years younger than me, I was her big brother, her protector and her trust in me was unwavering. I remember her first day in school. She was afraid, lost and clinching to my arm as to a buoy. She was drowning and I was her lifesaver. During few days, until she adjusted, I was seating in the kindergarten section of the classroom, next to her, a privilege granted to me by the teacher, who, according to my mother, said that "he has never seen a pupil as talented as I"!

Anyway, I did not want to move. I had my places where I played with my friends, building cabins made of branches of trees and of a bush called "genets" - in French - which grows in the cold, high altitude mountains. One place was called "the Hill", which was covered with big boulders at the bottom, where we were playing Indians and Cow-boys; another hill was called "the four pine trees" although there were never more than three (go figure!) where I liked to go to spend time with Monique; another "the skiers" because adults were skiing the slope in winter while we, the kids, were shooting down on our luges. Finally, "the plantation", an oak planted area which was providing shade and a relief from heat for our family pick-nicks in the midst of the hot summers. In addition to my commitment to school, I was also chosen by the priest to become an altar boy. So, after a brief training by the priest himself, I served my first mass at the age of six in the small church of Theix which the priest was tending one Sunday per month. By the age of seven I had settled in the village of Theix and the idea of moving was as good as living a nightmare. Once I confronted my parents just to be sure that I was not preoccupying myself for nothing. Unfortunately my fears became reality. My mother explained to me that the teacher talked to her and recommended that, for my sake, we all move to a place where some higher education was available. He said that I was to go far, as far as studying, and that she and my father should prepare to support me in this endeavor to the fullest extent of their ability! For my mother, answering the call of the teacher was her new mission. For my father it was another breakdown in the middle of a relatively good life. After almost four years of his life between the dairy plant and the pig farm, what he most dreaded was to leave his friends. They were a handful of other refugees. Among them was a Polish couple, another mixed Czech and Hungarian couple and a single Russian guy. Except for the Hungarian woman who spoke some Russian, all the others spoke in their native Slavic languages, which are very similar to Polish. For my father it was the first place in a foreign country where he could communicate with some ease, almost all the time, since his French was still mediocre.

The Polish family was the one from Chateau de Ravel whom my parents met when we lived in Chateau-Gaillard. Actually they were the ones who found a job for my parents at the dairy plant, after they, themselves, moved to Theix to work for a rich and affluent family composed of two single sisters. These two owned a pharmacy in Clermont-Ferrand, where they lived most of the time in an apartment, but also enjoyed their country house in Theix, usually on week-ends or during holidays. There, the Polish ones were acting as maid and servant, for the wife, and chauffeur and gardener for the husband. "Vladek", the husband, was educated, had a driver's license and was spending time in Clermont-Ferrand, chauffeuring the pharmacists, as was needed and then returning to the mansion in Theix to perform his less appealing duty as gardener. The Polish lived in a guest house located on the sisters' property. The other refugees were working at the dairy plant with my father and were also tending the pig farm which was an extension of the dairy plant since the pigs were fed, among other trashy foods, on milk leftovers. Less fortunate than my parents or the Vladek's family, they lived in shacks nearby the pig farm…

When we were invited by the Polish to spend Sundays with them, it was when the sisters were not at the mansion, so that we all could use the owners' huge dining room where the meals were served by the wives on a big table under an enormous chandelier. Before that house, I had never seen anything like that. To me, it was a castle and the furnishing and the decoration showed a wealth unknown to me until now. That was when I began to understand what being rich was. Not only that, but riding in the sisters' car, a traction 15 (the same as the one of the owner of Chateau-Gaillard), driven by Vladek, gave me a sense of superiority I have only experienced once before. It was when I was watching, fascinated in admiration, the delivery of two cars, ordered by the owner of the dairy plant, which were pulled in front of his house from a covered truck. One was a red "Buick" and the other one a light green "Chevrolet". Although none of these things belonged to me, I became infatuated with them by merely being around them. This is when I promised to myself that, one day, I will be rich too.

This new concept helped me to overcome the idea of moving again since the move was precisely linked to getting educated and therefore being able to get rich in return… For my father, I became the cause of his misery. He knew the move was for my sake and because of my mother's authoritative, non negotiable, decision, his only option was to keep his mouth shut and submit to her will.

CHAPTER 3

MISTER THE PRIEST (MONSIEUR LE CURE)

"Les Martres-de-Veyre" is a small town of approximately two thousand people in the "Limagne" plain between the volcanoes mountain chain, on the West, and the hilly woody region of "Vic-le-Comte", another town of about three thousand souls, on the East. Les Martres-de-Veyre is located approximately ten kilometers, South East of Clermont-Ferrand, just about the same distance Theix was in the South West.

At the farm, in their new jobs, my father was supposed to replace the aging supervisor and my mother his wife who was afflicted by a cancer of the throat. We moved to an apartment in a two story building own by the owner of the farm which was rented free to us, as a partial payment in nature, of their salaries. Money was not so great but, as unqualified workers, my parents could not be too picky as to the jobs being offered to them. Nevertheless the opportunity for schooling was much greater than what was offered in Theix. Few days after having moved, we had the unexpected visit of: "Monsieur le Cure" - "Mister the Priest" as he was referred to -, the Catholic priest of the parish of Les Martres-de-Veyre which comprised two other villages named "Corent" for one and "Mirefleurs" for the other. The man was tall, a little bold and dressed in a black cassock closing in the front with buttons (a lot of them) and cinched around his waist with a wide black belt knotted in the old fashion way. His appearance was very conservative as compared to modern priests who were given the choice to dress as civilians with pants and a jacket at the condition that the color was black or very dark grey. Obviously he was wearing the white hard collar and the huge cross around his neck that all priests were required to wear, no matter whether they were conservative or liberal. At that time of my life, priests were either wearing the outfits of Mister the priest or those of civilians or, in between, a cassock with a zipper instead of buttons and a clip-on belt instead of the knotted one. The latter was the outfit of the priest of Saint-Genes-Champanelle from whom I had just departed. Indeed our new priest was a true conservative. In the village, then, there were three authorities: the Mayor, the Teacher and the Priest. Nobody would have ever dared to question or challenge the legitimacy of their power whether it was obtained by the grace of God or the trust of the voters or the awesome respect for academic knowledge! The mayor, a Medical Doctor, was also a conservative and kept winning elections after elections. I have not seen another mayor, but him, for the twelve years of my stay in Les Martres-de-Veyre. The Doctor and the priest were allies, in principle, but were smart enough to behave as the mayor of all citizens and the priest of all parishioners. For the teacher, it was a different story. He was representing: "modernity", gained through knowledge, and therefore very critical of faith in an invisible God or submission to outdated traditions. This being said, he was the natural opponent of the forces of darkness which were still ruling this modern world of his! When I speak of the teacher, I am not referring to a person in particular but to a "prototype" who embraces the concept of atheism as a fundamental basis for the unlimited progress of humanity. A lot of them were socialists or communists since communism was the flourishing ideology of developing U.S.S.R. However, the teacher, as the mayor and the priest, was smart enough to behave in a way acceptable to all pupils' parents whether they were from the "right" or from the "left".

For my family and me, it became very clear, very quickly, that the real authority, in the village, was the priest. It did not take long before he enrolled me in his group of altar boys (twenty at all time, present at the solemn mass on Sundays, plus a reserve of few, just in case of unexpected, last minute, defections) and requested my presence to organize and police the Thursday afternoons "patronage". There I was, keeping the younger kids in line before entering the Presbyterian patronage room and then insuring their seating, girls on the left, boys on the right, and quietness during the projection of Christian motivational movies or slide shows. I was making sure that the room was clean before and after each event and that the priest's instructional materials were properly stored until the following Thursday. The main motivator of the patronage and of its big success was the "quatre-heure" or the four o'clock snack. It consisted of jelly and jam spread on slices of bread, chocolate bars and unlimited sodas. Almost all kids under the age of seven were attending. In school, I consolidated my position as "the first of the class" and kept it until I left the primary school to middle school which I attended in Clermont-Ferrand. My first class in primary school, in Les Martres-de-Veyre, was CE2 (Cours Elementaire

DEUXieme annee) or third grade with a teacher who used to call me: "casque d'or" (the golden helmet) because of the reddish gold color of my hair. I heard that he was a "Pied Noir" (Black Foot) repatriated from Algeria where he spent five years on a teaching contract to pay for his scholarship. I knew about the Indian tribe of Black Foot in America but could not make a connection between Algeria and America. On the other hand he was not red skinned as I imagined all Indians would be. Anyway, several years passed before I was explained that the "North African Black Foot" was the surname given to the white land owners of the French colonies of "Algeria", "Tunisia" and "Morocco" who were wearing rubber black boots.

Boys were on one side of the school building and the girls on the other side, separated by a big wall - at least eight feet tall - and communicating by a small plain steel door... rusted and always under locks! Gender segregation was in full swing and for a boy, to talk to a girl, in public, was reprehensible. Mixity was not even allowed at catechism. Boys were attending on Thursdays before noon while girls did it in the afternoon. It was only at the time of preparation for the solemn communion that, for the first time, boys and girls were put together to rehearse the procession from the back of the church to the altar, boys on the right side of the nave and girls on the left side of it. Position in the procession was decided by a final catechism exam. The good grades were in the front while the bad ones were in the back. It happened that, here too, I was "the first of the class" and, as such, I was leading the procession for the boys. As for the girls, "Carmen", of Portuguese descents, led the girls. She was in love with me, but I was not. My secret love was "Josiane", the second of the class whose eyes were all on another boy and not so much on me, although we were friendly to each other if not "bonamis" as I wished we would be! Anyway, in spite of official segregation, as anyone could imagine, boys and girls had their ways to meet in places which were known to all but never mentioned, publicly, by anyone. That is where the kissing, the touching, the cuddling and fumbling were practiced by "apprentices" of the art of love! Consummation of the sexual act was rare since the girls had no access to contraceptive pills neither boys to condoms and, in case of unwanted pregnancy, no one wished to be categorized as "bad" girl or boy or worse: being finger-pointed and labeled "perverts" by the whole village. It was in one of these semi-private settings that I discovered, to my chagrin that Josiane was not for me. My love, or shall I say, lust for her, was platonic and lasted until I left the primary school and went to middle/high school in Clermont-Ferrand.

My parents did not get the job promised at the farm. The current supervisor and his wife were surviving beyond the morbid expectations of the owner. So, after three years in the farm, they changed jobs again, but remained in the village. This change caused another move further down the street from where we lived. The new place was called: "le couvent" - the convent - because it was a real one at some point in time, but one day, the few remaining sisters left it to join another declining community nearby and sold the building to the municipality, which, in turn, transformed it into apartments for the needy. So there we were, in the convent, with indoor plumbing for running water, sewage and toilets; all of this outside the apartment but on the same floor. We were two families per floor to share the utilities. In addition to the apartment, the rent came with a piece of garden, just about half an acre in size. As far as the utilities go, it was not a surprise at all since we had similar accommodations in the previous housing… needless to say it was far from the comfort enjoyed by the privileged middle-class population around us. Waste water was flowing from the sewage sink inside to a ditch dug on both sides of the street outside. Concerning the toilets, here in the new apartment, we were saved from emptying our night pots in an outhouse outside the building... and that was a real progress, especially in winter! Finally, in terms of hygiene, dad and I kept going to the municipal shower room, for men only, once a week, on Saturdays, while the girls were bathing at home, in a portable tube, which was filled with hot boiling water from the coal stove tank in the kitchen. That furnace was the most precious piece of furniture, besides the beds... and the tube. There my mother was cooking and it was also the only source for heating during the long cold winter days...

In his new job, my father was the "gofer" in a team of a dozen of masons, brick and stone layers and carpenters. The boss man was a rich entrepreneur who was paying well to keep his business alive, since he was the only "registered and insured" official and legal builder in the area, but was seriously challenged by a couple of Italian and Spanish immigrants who were working in the shadows of the black market, stealing contracts and qualified labor from him. The boss man was a short stocky man with a big belly. Some said he got it because of too much wine drinking and that his liver has developed a disease called: "cirosis". He liked partying and entertaining his crew of workers every Saturdays with a barbeque and a lot of wine and gnole. As expected my father was returning home from these libations, drunk and ready to pick a fight with my mother who, since he started to work for the builder, was in a state of chronic anger with him.

What happened during our first years at the "convent" is hardly believable. My mother became pregnant twice and delivered a girl first, by the name of: "Brigitte", nine years younger than me, and then a boy: "Jean-Marc", eleven years younger! For my older sister Christine and me these two additions were unwelcome and very quickly started to suck to much air from our environment. Although we were respectful of them as brother and sister, the added chores which came with their presence were far from keeping us happy, and at times, we wished they were not there! Although it was not a death wish, my little sister died at the age of nine months from a poorly treated case of measles. In spite of all the respect my mother had for the Doctor, who, by the way, admitted his incompetence to cure my sister, she made an appointment with a "witch doctor" that had a talk show on the radio. The talk show host became my mother's new God for a while… but lost his godly status when my sister died. Needless to say that the whole family was devastated and the entire village was assembled in the church, too small to dwell all the people who wanted to pay their respect to my parents. At the end of the funeral mass, my parents, my sister and me on their side, were receiving the condolences of the village standing in front of a minuscule white coffin covered with white flowers. With us, but a couple of steps behind, were the priest and the Doctor.

This moment was so overwhelming that, a couple of years later, my sister and I never bristle anymore when my mother was asking us to take little brother for a walk, in his stroller, in the open air which was supposed to help him with a chronic whopping cough. At home life was sad for awhile. In order to forget (assuming this was the real reason) my father was getting home drunk, most every day, and my mother's anger was growing proportionately with my father's drunkenness. When a sudden scene was breaking out, and since we had no personal privacy in the house, my sister and I were escaping from the home fouled atmosphere by going to the garden, on the pretence of being busy, in order to avoid witnessing their verbal fights. The garden was, at the same time, a hidden refuge but also our "forced labor camp" since it was our job to water the plants, remove the weeds and harvest, whatever was ripe at any given time, from spring to fall. Everybody knew about the Wnuk's garden where people were shopping directly from the producer to the consumer. In addition to produce, my mother was also growing poultry and rabbits. The quality of the eggs, not to speak of the quality of the meat, was second to none. Mother was making good money with her garden, even at times, more than my father's weekly wages. As for my sister and I, we have developed, during these years, such a hate for agriculture that I promised myself to never come close to gardening when I grow old. With money beginning to flow more abundantly than ever before, mother decided to move to a bigger and more comfortable apartment located on main-street. There we had a full floor for us alone ending on one side with a balcony as wide as the whole building. Running water, underground sewage and private toilets were all ours, not to share with anybody else. The only thing missing was a private shower. Because of that, father and I kept going to the public showers and the portable tube was not yet decommissioned. It is at this new address that we acquired our first TV set. I was ten years old when it happened. The dictatorial control of the "machine" was my mother's duty and she excelled at using it as a disciplinary tool as well... At this time there was just one channel in black and white with news at 12:00 noon, for half an hour, and then nothing till 5:00pm when games (like jeopardy) began, followed by the news at 7:00pm and documentaries until 9:00pm by which time kids were supposed to go to bed or leave the TV room. Beginning at 9:00pm was either a taped staged comedy or drama show or a sporting event or a news report or a movie. There were no ads and a "speakrine" was appearing between programs to present and summarize the next one. Some movies were shown with a white square at the bottom right of the screen meaning that the movie was rated "R" and was unsuitable for kids' viewing under the age of eighteen. As far as I am concerned, there was no viewing of such movies, along with my parents, even when I was eighteen! The lengthier programs were running on Thursdays and Sundays and ran uninterrupted from 10:00am on Sundays, beginning with the Catholic mass and from 12:00 noon, non-stop, on Thursdays, with kids' stuff the whole afternoon, until the evening news. The popular expansion of TV made our priest pissed off because both the Sundays' and Thursdays' programming made some older parishioners took advantage of having mass at home to skip going to church and the attendance of the younger ones at the patronage grew weaker…

CHAPTER 4

"MICHELIN" AND THE AMERICAN CARTOONS

I was approaching my 11th birthday when talks about my future schooling were again taking center stage in my parents' conversations. My mother became so much obsessed about it that no other discussions were possible between the two of them. Finally, after a little while and suspecting that ultimately there were a job change and/or a move at stake, my father could not stand it anymore and was shutting her down as soon as my mother was opening her mouth, by mocking her ambition to make of me a: "director" (in his imaginary: somebody wearing a three piece suite with a white shirt and a tie). My father's idea of me, after finishing primary school, was to work as an apprentice at his employer's business and become a mason or a skilled craftsman in any other trades being practiced by his construction company. My mother hated these manual menial my ambitious mother. Consequently my mother went head-on for naturalization as soon as she understood the need and we became all French... no more Polish or Apatride! When the priest scheduled another foreign trip, this time to Italy, mainly to Turin where was exposed the shroud in which Jesus was buried, there was no need for me for special permission to cross the border. Like all other altar boys, I had my French I.D. (National Identity Card) right with me, in my wallet, stuck into the rear pocket of my jeans...

During my twelve years in les Martres-de-Veyre, and thanks to the priest, I had visited most of all regions in France and also went abroad to Switzerland and Italy. Until today, I believe that the priest was the one who has inoculated the virus of travel in my blood! Of all the trips, the one to Italy remains the most memorable because of the shroud in which Jesus was buried. As it was explained to us, on site, the rectangular shroud was folded in two along its length and Christ was laid onto it such that his whole body was covering one half of the length, feet close to one edge and the head near the middle towards the opposite edge, and was recovered by the other half across his head down to his feet. According to experts' reports and scientific testing of the shroud, the body of Christ, being covered with balm and oily fragrance, impregnated the fabric of the shroud which, much later under the heat of a fire, from which it was rescued, produced a negative picture of his body, front and back, due to the way he was wrapped in. In the cathedral of Turin, the unfolded shroud was protected by a glass frame and shown entirely with the back side of Christ on the left of the frame and the front on the right, the two sides being symmetrical to the center of the shroud. At first I saw nothing, just a bunch of black and white and also brown spots and lines. I started to concentrate where the face of Christ should be. All of a sudden I was in stupor. I was seeing all the details of his holy face in negative... It took my breath away!

jobs which, in her opinion, were keeping the working class in relative poverty. Of course she wanted me to become an educated man wearing a white shirt and a tie at all times, during the week days, at work, and not only on Sundays like some did, at mass, to impress their fellow parishioners.

The priest was thinking about my education as well. At the end of the 5th grade, the choice for the pupils was either to add three more years in primary school and pass an exam that would grant them a "certificate of education" (very well valued at that time) and then go to work on apprenticeship, which lasted three years, before being graduated in their trade, or to go to "college" (middle high/high school until 10th grade) to get a secondary education which begins in the 6th grade. The priest's interest in my education was about making a priest of me. So, being of age, it was time to send me to a seminary and begin a curriculum similar to the one taught in lay colleges along with the specific teachings leading to priesthood. My sustained status of "first of the class" in school as well as my piety for the things of the church not to mention my unquestionable availability to the priest, were the assets being looked for to become all at once: a representative of Christ on earth, a servant of humanity and a devoted and obedient clergyman.

One day, after mass, he approached me and asked me blankly if I wanted to become a priest. Before I could answer, he started to talk about a seminary nearby in "Courpiere", known of me, where his nephew, a friend of mine, was in his second year. When he stopped after a couple of minutes which seemed to have lasted two hours, he was waiting for my answer. It was: NO! To my surprise he did not pursue the conversation to either know why, or ask for explanations. He just changed subject and reminded me to be on time for the evening vespers and that he also needed me, after the service, to count and package the proceeds of the collections at the morning masses. The packaging consisted in rolling the coins in bank wrappings and unfolding and flattening the bills before enclosing them in envelopes. That Sunday, when I did not heed the call, was just like any other Sunday! Few Sundays after this uneventful one, returning home after vespers, I found my parents in a heated verbal fight again which I did not understand at first since it was about a certain: "Michelin". I did not know who or what Michelin was, or what it was about it and therefore what was all that fuss for! As soon as they saw me, they calmed down. My father took his hat and went out. My mother asked me to sit down and, very ceremonially, told me that she had to talk to me. That was an event since in normal exchanges with her I was mostly taking orders without discussion or, otherwise, talking about my progress in school, her favorite subject! What she had to say was that the priest has found a job for my father at Michelin, which is a tire manufacturing business, in Clermont-Ferrand. At that point I understood what Michelin was, not knowing yet if it was the name of a person or of a company, and was not surprised a bit that mother wanted father to make more money and also to get out of the vicious company of his current employer and his drunken click… My mother told me that "Mr. Michelin" was the owner of his tire manufacturing company and, in his benevolence he was also providing education in his private schools: pre-schools, primary schools, colleges as well as vocational schools for craftsmen and technicians and graduate schools for engineers. These schools were for employees' children exclusively and therefore, since the hiring of my father, one way or another, my education was warranted if I demonstrated the aptitudes required to become a professional. For my mother it was a blessing from God (or the priest who was honored as God). For her my future was crystal clear. She wanted me to become anything less but an engineer and she believed, without the shadow of a doubt, that I would succeed.

I passed the one full day exam for admission in the 6th grade and began to go to school at "college d'enseignement general CHARRAS" - named after a local politician - at the next back to school session in September. From that moment on I was spending more time in Clermont-Ferrand than in les Martres-de-Veyre. I was still a pillar of the church during the week-ends but my real life was in town… Actually a big town!

My mother decided, without asking me, that I will be an engineer, because she knew better what was best for me and, besides, for her, that was the only good option available at that time. I knew that she knew about the priest's proposal to make me a priest but she did not mention it since, in her eyes, the alternative with Michelin looked so much better in spite of the prestige of priesthood!

Except for the first year, I was riding the train from les Martres-de-Veyre to Clermont-Ferrand, a twenty minute ride with two stops. Riding the train became such an uneventful routine that I was going with the flow without paying any attention to what was going on. In the train, we were sitting in clans and the whole train was noisy with the chats of the kids. Here, girls and boys were mixed-up until we reached school, just about ten minutes away from the train station, by foot. There, gender discrimination was again in effect.

During the first year I drove to Clermont-Ferrand by car with an engineer at Michelin, and his two sons who were also attending college CHARRAS. Mother almost begged him to take me with his sons since she was scared to death that I won't be able to take the train alone or find my way to school from the train station in Clermont-Ferrand… She would have loved to stay with this arrangement for ever but one day the engineer persuaded her that I and his sons were big enough to take the train alone. The first day it did happen, she must have been dying from fear of not being in control. After a while she got used to it but claimed assuredly, that everybody, including myself, were in harms' way with all of these malicious people riding along with us. Mother was very possessive and protective, more with me than with my sister or my younger brother. I was the flagship of the family and my success was her success, therefore, as a precious jewel, I was to be protected from all dangers, real or perceived. At my age, obeying was a second nature and for that I was talked about as the perfect son all mothers dreamt to have!

In retrospect, at that time of my life, the idea of moving to or living in America was as foreign a concept as imagining a man walking on the moon... Though it did happen! Nevertheless America was not completely foreign to me. Each week I was going to the news store to buy comic strips romancing the stories of "Kit Carson", "Buffalo Bill", "Hopalong Cassidy", "Buck Jones", "Davy Crocket" and many others. Holding the precious books in my hands was the happiest moment of the week. I was collecting them religiously and was spending hours reading and re-reading them and scrutinizing the drawings depicting the heroic prowess of these characters. Sometimes I was dreaming of joining them in the desert of "Arizona" or the snowy mountains of the "Sierra Nevada" or the arches of "Utah" or the ranches of "Texas" or the valleys of "Oklahoma"... Even at times I regretted not having embraced the carrier of priesthood since I was told that a lot of priests were sent to North America, as missionaries, to evangelize the Indians. At that time of my life, playing "cowboys and Indians" was the game in vogue. Although I played it earlier around the boulders of the hill in Theix, now, thanks to the cartoons, I had some sort of academic knowledge of my distant heroes. My surname was: "Buck Jones". I was leading a bunch of a dozen of kids in battles to defeat other groups and destroy their camps. In our childish eyes, the hills around les Martres-de-Veyre were bigger than the "Rockies" and the gorges of the river "Allier", our "Red River" between Texas and Oklahoma, deeper than the "Grand Canyon" itself. Needless to say that all the courage and bravery we had displayed in the battle fields were mocked, ridiculed and turned to ashes by our mothers when they saw us returning home, in the evening, with bruises, bloody noses, torn clothes and smelling smoke from bone fires. In spite of the punishments for bad behavior, it was worth to live it and we were just patiently waiting until our mothers forgot, or pretended to, to plan the next battle…

I have lived in les Martres-de-Veyre for twelve years, from the age of seven to the age of nineteen. Until I reached the age of twelve, I did not know that I was not French. I knew that my parents were deported from Poland, spent time in German forced labor camps during WWII and immigrated to France as U.N. refugees but all of that, in my mind, did not have anything to do with the fact of being French or not! The discovery of the status of my citizenship was revealed to me, by the priest, the year he planned for the altar boys to take a trip to: "Switzerland".

Before going any further, I would like to elaborate a little bit about the trips. Every year the altar boys were doing fund raising in the parish in order to pay for a cultural trip organized by the priest and the elders of at least fifteen years of age. In addition to raising funds, two or three Sunday collections were usually added to cover the entire cost of the trips. These trips were the priest's way of rewarding us for the church services and also the occasion to teach us, for a week, on a daily basis, facts of life such as organization, teamwork, discipline and responsibility. In addition, each trip had a theme and he was eager to teach history and geography on site.

Needless to say that I was French until the priest told me otherwise. For him it did not seem to be a big deal, since just about 20% of the population of the village was issued from immigration after WWII, but for me it was. I was living in France, going to a French school, spoke French, prayed in French, so what was he talking about? Everything about me was French, even my first name: "Bernard"… Unfortunately, for the first time, to my great chagrin, I came to realize that my first name was not Bernard but "Bogdan" and this was the name by which I was identified in the papers that the priest had to file for me in order to obtain a foreigner's visa to enter Switzerland. Bernard was the name of the elder son of the owners of Chateau-Gaillard and the wife of the owner suggested to my mother to call me Bernard (because it began with a "B" as in Bogdan and Bernard) in order to sound more French, and so she did. Last but not least, my citizenship was: "apatride" meaning a person without country. At that point I was stoned.

CHAPTER 5

THE TRAVELING "APATRIDE"

My mother tried, with a lot of effort, to mitigate the impact of these revelations on me. At the end we were both speechless. Me not knowing what to ask for and her staying silent so that no more hidden things were brought to light. My mother was very secretive and she hated to talk about the country and the people that she left behind. It was only by pure chance that I found out that she came from a wealthy family from Krakow, that her academic studies, to become a professor, were cut short when she was caught by the Nazis and deported to Germany while demonstrating with other students in Warszawa at the gates of what will become later the: "Jewish ghetto" of Warszawa. Some of this information was overheard when we had company, at coffee time, when kids have left the dining table to play around. I also heard, once, that she had a sister but did interrupt the relation with her when she started demanding too much of my mother, who, by all accounts, at that time, was living in one of the "richest" war devastated country in Europe. As for my father, I just learned that he was the seventh son of a family of seven living on the proceeds of a farm near Kalisz, when my mother was nagging him about his low upbringing! Even, it was only much later that I learned of their birthplaces, for her in Czestochowa (the Holiest place in Poland for Catholics) and for him in Russow-Tekadow (the most red-neck, uneducated place in rural Poland). This happened when we were preparing the papers for naturalization. At that moment again I was told that, due to my status of apatride, I did not have to take the French citizenship, along with my parents, since such a status granted me the choice of becoming a citizen of any nation belonging to the United Nations, by the age of twenty one. At that time, the lawyer who represented me, as a minor of sixteen years, explained to me that, concerning citizenship, some countries had a "right of blood" and others a "right of land". These rights would determine which nationality a person would bear at birth. As an example, if a child was born of foreigners in a country with the right of blood, the child was given the citizenship of the parents (which is that of the father since, in these times, birth out of wedlock was almost inconceivable… or unspoken of!). However if a child was born of foreigners, in a country with the right of land, the child was given the nationality of the country of birth. In my case, in order to meet the "apatride international legal requirements" it was necessary that I lived in a foreign country (France), was born of foreign parents (Polish) in a "no man's land" (Germany) - which was occupied by powers foreign to that land and therefore not considered as a sovereign country -. Most apatride statuses were granted to children of war. The occupying powers in Germany were the allied forces of the USA, Great Britain and France in West Germany - not to mention the USSR, in East Germany - under the U.N. administration making

Germany an occupied territory but not a sovereign country. So, my sister and brother, all born in France from Polish parents, were Polish because France had a right of blood and became French by "filiation" (meaning taking the citizenship of the parents with no personal involvement as minors). As for me, I became French by naturalization (meaning taking the citizenship by choice). Even as a minor, I became French on my own volition with, as mentioned earlier, the assistance of the lawyer who represented me before the Judge. Thus, at the age of sixteen I became officially French although, in my heart, I was always French and, for ever, will be. The episode of naturalization took place at the end of my scholarship in College CHARRAS, equivalent to the tenth grade in the USA.

At that junction, students had the choice to complete a High School degree called "Baccalaureate" by going to a "lycee" (a two years school preparing for universities) or quit right there their secondary education and opt for a professional curriculum which, in the case of a technical orientation, would grant students a diploma equivalent to a BS degree (bachelor of science) in engineering fields, five years down the road. Because the Michelin private schools' curriculum did not offer the former baccalaureate, I was set to follow the latter professional path. Although studies in France and in the U.S. are sliced and diced differently, let's just say that a BS student from a US university would certainly compete successfully with a low ranking French engineer fresh from school.

The reason why naturalization happened at that time is because the director of E.E.T.M. (Ecole d'Enseignement Technique Michelin - Michelin private Technical College -), which I was to attend at the completion of the tenth grade, explained to my mother that I could be denied jobs in government related activities if I was not French. The private sector did not have such requirements but alienating the public sector from access was unacceptable for

I could not take my eyes from him. I have never been that close to God. From then on, this image never quit obsessing me. At last, then, I was in the presence of the "superman" of whom the monk, in Theix, spoke so eloquently for the St. Nicholas' feast.

Along with the bus trips, the priest had also some other tricks in his bag to keep us motivated by the Christian lifestyle as opposed to, as he said: the "playboy" lifestyle. The next popular one was a week-long trekking in the wilderness of the most deserted region of France. Each year, the selected bunch, with good health and strong legs was transported by train to a remote location somewhere in the middle of nowhere and slated to join another train station one hundred miles further in seven days. From year to year, the arrivals and departures places where different but what remained unchanged were the overall distance (give and take few miles), the duration and the region which covered the "departments" (size wise equivalent to US counties) of "Lozere", "Ardeche", "Aveyron" and "Cantal"… a.k.a. the "French desert"! It was there mainly that the French military were testing weapons and practicing warfare in the training camps of "Larsac". Also spotted, here and there, were farms and monasteries which we used as resting and feeding places at the end of each legs of the trail. On these trips, we learned the agonizing pain of pushing ourselves to the limits and the joy of stopping and resting in the warmth of stables smelling the typical odor of hay and cows. Each day, the sense of accomplishment was so overwhelming that all pains were gone in no time. We were living on the local inhabitants who knew we were coming. The food was simple: bread, eggs, bacon, ham, soup, cheese and fruits (mostly apples). The bedding consisted of our own sleeping bags and the hay that was stored in the barn above the cows. One of our challenges before each trip was to write to the priests of the parishes we were to stay at and ask them for assistance in finding and convincing helpful Christian peasants to shelter and feed us! Writing to an adult stranger when you are fifteen was very intimidating. At that time only the postal service was widely available for written correspondences. We had no internet for instant replies to our requests. We had to wait for days and sometimes weeks before getting an answer. As strange as it might be, we have never received a negative response. In retrospect, I wondered if the priest, or more precisely his telephone, had anything to do with that! Anyway, if it did, the game was well played and we were left with the feeling of having achieved something great. Job well done, used to say the priest, when we were receiving a positive answer and, keep-up with the good work, when we were sweating our brains to formulate the best way to ask for help, which, by our standards, could never be: NO! From year to year, new faces were showing up whereas older ones were disappearing but the bunch was always made of approximately fifteen guys (no girls allowed).

The third trick was to retreat, in full seclusion, in monasteries, living for four days and three nights the life of monks. The two places I will never forget are: "l'Abbaye De Sept-Fonts" and "Notre Dame Des Neiges". One monastery was producing "vegetaline", a nutrient extracted from wheat, and the other a sparkling pink wine called: "la fleur des neiges" (the flower of the snow). The former was located in the plain of Limagne and the latter in the forested mountains of Lozere. Living like monks and following them in their daily tasks was taking rapidly an unusual toll on us, especially at night when we were to get up every three hours and pray for fifteen minutes before returning to bed… yet, on the third night, this routine became almost an addictive habit or a new challenging lifestyle which, at the end of the stay, we were quitting with sour regrets. These three events (the touristic bus trips, desert trekking and monastic retreats) were evenly distributed over the three months of summer vacation so that there was always something exiting to expect each month. In between, we were, more or less, resuming our battles of cow-boys and Indians, however, by the age of fourteen these kids games started to fade away and, consequently, friends and foes united, we were more often going fishing or bicycling together, activities which contributed to cement our small town friendship.

The last trip to Abbey De Sept Fonds took place when I was eighteen. On that year, I passed my driving license and, my parents who never had a car, bought a superb vintage "Citroen traction 11BL" from 1947 which owner was a respected and respectable retired military "colonel". Due to the reputation of the colonel, no one would have ever imagined that he could have sold a lemon, especially to a young man like me and under the watch of the priest. Nevertheless, in the end, it looked like a lemon whether he had any knowledge of it or not! But NO, actually, I was the lemon! Although it was well known that checking the oil gauge was as important as checking the gas gauge before any long trip, I failed to do so, for the oil, at the beginning of the two hundred kilometers trip to the monastery… and the car failed me five kilometers short from getting there! The engine seized due to a lack of proper lubrication. It was a big blow to me, especially when one studies mechanical engineering. Fortunately I managed to sell the car at a local service station where the car was towed in and, "holy cow" I sold it to an amateur of old Citroen cars, twice the price my parents bought it… Since for the buyer-collector, price was not an issue, I was told later that I could have sold it for more. But, all things considered, I was a happy camper. Few phone calls from the service station brought two devoted parishioners from Les Martres de Veyre to pick us up in the afternoon of that day. The stay at the monastery was cancelled and we were all safe and happy to be back at home, that same day, late at night. When I arrived at home, my mother was livid. Before she could utter a word, I showed her the money I made for the sale and that brought back to her face the obsequious smile she was wearing when she was talking to people above her class level. This time I decided to buy the replacement car without her participation. My counselors were the assurance agent from "Vic-le-Comte" and a car mechanic who lived in the same building as us, one story above. According to them, I needed to buy a German car. Based on the money available, I could afford an "Opel Record" made by "Opel", a subsidiary of the American company "General Motors". With the money left over, I was able to pay the increased insurance fees for a year. The used car dealer was a friend of the assurance agent and that, in and by itself, greatly facilitated the transaction. After test-driving it, the neighbor mechanic swore to me that the car was a jewel!

In retrospect, I wonder if the car, manufactured in Germany - my place of birth - by an American car maker, was not a forerunner sign of my future in the U.S.A!

CHAPTER 6
ON THE WAY TO CLERMONT-FERRAND

In addition of being secretive, possessive and protective, my mother was also very ambitious. She never claimed this value for herself but wanted to achieve it through me. She believed that my success in life would bring her power and glory. She saw herself as the "king maker" that everybody would bless for her "creation". In order to progress in this direction she needed advice and support. Naturally she turned to the priest.

The priest explained to her, in details, that Michelin, the provider of a job to my father and free schooling to my sister, brother and me, was also a benevolent employer who was giving away free healthcare to its employees and families in its many dispensaries and clinics in Clermont-Ferrand, discounted produce and goods throughout its many exclusive stores in town, free burials and free social services such as almost free lodging in social housing with reduced costs for utilities and low cost meals in its huge restaurant built near the factory… Mother wanted to have access to "Michelin's providence", also known, politically as: "paternalism" which was only available in Clermont-Ferrand. To this effect she arranged, with the priest, to have a Michelin social worker to visit her and discuss her needs. For my mother it was crystal clear that benefiting from all these advantages will boost up the burgeoning financial wealth she was nurturing with care and that it would contribute to my personal material and intellectual growth!

The first meeting took place on a Saturday afternoon and, since we were out of school, it happened that not only the parents but the kids as well were present at the meeting.

The dining room table was full of goodies: cakes, chocolates, etc… tea, coffee and soft drinks. She was right on time, at two pm, on the dot! At first everybody was surprised to see a "petite", looking like in her sixteen, introducing herself as: "Anne-Marie", the social worker from Michelin. She was dynamic, very friendly and her smile was contagious… No, she was not sixteen but twenty one and on her first assignment after graduating from the Michelin training center for social services. The first ten or fifteen minutes were about her, her family and how she ended up at the training center after failing the baccalaureate… then began the unbelievable saga of the Wnuk's family from Poland to France via Nazi Germany. My mother was good at narrating the exodus in general terms without getting really too personal. During the conversation I heard that, at the nearing end of the war, when Hitler was desperate and wanted to kill as many people as the extermination camps could handle, that my mother and a couple of other Polish girls, were removed from their forced labor factory and awaiting to be loaded in a train to "Auschwitz" when a Polish speaking German soldier overheard them speaking Polish and lamenting that, not only the Jews but also Catholics were destined to extermination... When they claimed they were not Jew, they were motioned out of the line and sent back to the factory where their assumed religion was verified and shortly after re-assigned to their former jobs while the others were climbing the cattle railcars to their final destination. This event, overtime, was repeated and dramatized to the point that many, in our extended family, still believe that my mother spent the duration of the war in a concentration camp where I was supposedly born as well!

My father was silent, politely sipping coffee. My sister and brother excused themselves and moved to the kitchen to watch TV. My father finally found the pretext of something to do and also left the table. Now we were just the three of us and my mother started to talk about me. She explained how good of a son I was and proclaimed that she and my father would have never survived had I not been with them at all times, all the way, translating, talking in their behalf and teaching them French. Her compliments about my skills and my dedication to them in front of a girl, almost my age, made me uncomfortable and I blushed more than once. On the other hand, Anne-Marie was questioning me as for a job interview. She seemed tireless to hear about my likes and dislikes, my plans for the future and even, discretely, asked if I had a girlfriend! This time my mother blushed also and rushed to my rescue with a resounding definitive: "certainly not"! I was at the center of the conversation and I was eighteen.

Few weeks after the meeting my parents were granted a condominium in one of the Michelin housing complexes in Clermont-Ferrand in the district of "Lachaux". Moving was on the order again...

Since the meeting, I kept thinking about Anne-Marie, who, with all due respect to her job, was nevertheless a pretty sexy prey that I would love to go after. She reminded me of the cartoon character: "Betty Boop", short hair, petite, plump with a mischievous demeanor which was an invitation to flirt.

At that time of my life, my sexual education was close to null since neither the church nor the school wanted to touch it with a ten foot pole. The subject was taboo and all in the education business including parents, mentors, teachers and priests seemed to agree that only "nature" and "life" should be the ultimate coaches of that touchy matter! For me it consisted mainly of my exposure to nude magazines and X-rated literature from the newspaper stand at the train station in Clermont-Ferrand and locker room's dirty talks with my athletic team mates. From the pornographic materials I could put my hands on and consisting of pictures of enticing naked women, torrid erotic literature and my own sexual fantasies about women, I made up my own idea about what women's attitude towards sex should be and how to fulfill their sexual pleasure during a sexual intercourse! From my point of view, I was persuaded that women were "hot erotic beings" endowed at birth with a "sex appeal" designed to attract males for procreation but, at the same time, to satisfy their sexual appetites, exacerbated by the urge to procreate. I saw these appetites comparable, if not stronger, as the males' ones. I was convinced, as far as sex is concerned, that they were egotistic self centered creatures, always looking for their own pleasure first, assuming or even knowing for sure, that their lust-obsessed male partners would always satisfy themselves one way or the other while making love…

Well, at that point, chasing Anne-Marie was out of question considering her involvement in our family affairs. Since Monique, my puppy love and Josiane whom I lusted after and loved platonically, the other girls I have met before and after meeting my future wife (including her for a short while) were merely "trophies" who were losing their attractiveness as soon as they were conquered. The conquest was the name of the game and sexual gratification was the price of victory. I was not so much interested in girls for their specific feminine attributes relative to intuition, emotion or sensuality, although I liked that in them, and for that have always respected them as special persons, but for their elusive quality of sexual attractiveness. This attraction had the power to tease and excite me and, while under its power, put me in a state of self centered bliss... like: "Nirvana"! In other more crude words, since nature had completed the "wiring" and "powering" of my genitals to the brain, the paramount pleasure was to feel the slow hardening of my penis while I was thinking of them or looking at them or chasing them or, in the midst of a romantic intercourse, preparing them for their own pleasure. In short, my fantasized understanding of women's sexuality was lust... not love! Therefore, during the foreplays I was leading them gently to accompany my intimate caresses and then letting them take over my lead and continue on, to masturbate on their own, till they reached orgasm. Looking at them thriving for pleasure and then losing control was sublime and, as expected, made me ejaculate my "brains" out! The sex games were deeply erotic, looming at the frontier of soft pornography which was the line not to cross in order to keep them coming back for more! Nevertheless, the more licentious the better!

    When meeting a new girl, my strategy was to pretend that I was not interested in having sex with her. Instead, I was concentrating my talking skills and seduction talents to convince her of her irresistible attractiveness to me and that my intentions were only to win her friendship. If, by chance, she bought into, or pretended to, my good hearted intentions the conversation then became more romantic. My next move was to question them and talk them into recreational sex and, along with it, the practice of safe sexual games which would bring pleasure without undesired consequences. I always insisted that by pleasing themselves first they would make me enjoy them even more… until I could satisfy myself. Consensual masturbation, including oral sex, which I was always initiating and loved to practice on them, with or without reciprocation, as a bonus, while they were masturbating frantically, was the safe goal of the lengthy times spent together on the back seat of my steamy car on cold days or on a blanket in the countryside under the starry skies on hot days. I knew instinctively that in the heat of the action my girls' need for sexual intercourse, if so desired, was as great as my desire to cleave them and, if not desired, in order to avoid pregnancy, oral or manual masturbation were good enough, as a substitute, to achieve orgasm. My tactic, on the other hand, was to always project the "3A" attitude of the guy being: Approachable, Agreeable and Available at all times. In other words creating an environment where she needed me more than I needed her. Putting the strategy and the tactic together has always worked. Girls were chasing me and tacitly begging for my company. I did not!

Having a car was very helpful in the hunt for girls and was providing a prestige and a sense of wealth which was not negligible in the eyes of not only girls but also of other less privileged neighbors. The car, however, was also a curse and a pain in the neck because I was the chauffeur of the family, namely: the chauffeur of my mother who was deciding when the car was to be used. While still living in Les Martres-de-Veyre, I had it sometimes during daylight on weekdays to drive to school in lieu of riding the train, but mainly on Saturdays and Sundays to take "mother and company" out for shopping on Saturdays and for a tour in the countryside on Sundays, after mass and the traditional Sunday meal taken at the dining room table (not the kitchen). Anyway, it was good to drive the family car in spite of my limited access to the vehicle. Twice we went on vacation to the beaches on the "Atlantic Ocean" with our neighbors. Camping in tents was very popular and the two families were enjoying each other very much. For the neighbors as for my parents, seeing the ocean was the event of their lifetime. Not so much for me since I had already spent one month on the ocean in a summer camp for under privileged kids when I was ten years old.

    Since the attribution of the condo, the idea of leaving my village for the big town was saddening me more than I could admit. It was in Les Martres-de-Vere that my senses grew up and matured. That is where my eyes were the clearest, my ears most finely tuned, my sense of smell and taste second to none; and the feel of the wind, the sun, the rain or snow, as well as the sensation of heat or cold on my skin were as real as a human touch! The whole world was concentrated in the microcosm of the village and its surrounding countryside. Mother-nature was generous with its changing seasons which I kept enjoying, year after year, always discovering something new along the trails in the hills or by the river. I loved walking by myself alone for hours. My body never tired and my mind wandering in dimensions where I had no control. During these walks, everything that I have lived and was living was coming back in flashes which kept disappearing as soon as I was about to capture and nurture them for a moment. The most obsessive one was that of "Superman Jesus". Not the one of the parish I was attending to. That one, unfortunately, sounded more like a dictator and a boring administrator, with reference to the priest's teachings, but the one of the monk in Theix. That one was emotional, sensual, spellbinding, fascinating beyond imagination, mindboggling and I decided to pursue Him until I found a satisfactory explanation to His attraction! Beside walking and bicycling, reading was my favorite pastime. Therefore, although I had some knowledge of God through catechism and creation (mainly through nature, the part of it accessible to humans), I decided to discover more of Him in books. At first, the dichotomy between Jesus the Son, so much real, human and humble, and God the Father so omnipotent, omniscient and omnipresent, made me looking for God away from Jesus as if He was not God Himself. I was soon seeking God in all the wrong places where Jesus was not. Among others, I engulfed myself in readings about the Egyptian, Greek and Latin mythologies and about the primitive cultures of the Americas. For the latter it covered the North-American Indian worshippers of the Great "Manito" Spirit, the "Aztecs" and the "Mayas" of Central America and the "Nazcas" and the "Incas" of South America. After trying hard to understand the incomprehensible, I redirected my interest to Jesus the man and His Godly human nature. Sometimes my professors were surprised to see me seating during recreations, in the library of the school, studying the "synoptic gospels" of Father "Theillard-de-Chardin" or tearing my emotions out while reading the French version of the novel: "The greatest story ever told" by "Fulton Oursher". My thirst for knowledge was inextinguishable and what started in Theix still follows me… The pursuit is still on and the excitement as vivid as when I was five years old or so.

Another thing that impacted my life was the discovery of photography. At College: CHARRAS, our professor of physics and chemistry was also volunteering to run a photo-club for students. The club was located near the chemistry amphitheater. The technology of the equipment was at the top level since he, himself, was a great fan of photography. At the time, the photo-lab was only equipped to make black and white pictures, which, as he said, was the best, if not the only way to create art-photographs. Rapidly I became his second in charge which granted me the privilege of carrying a key of the lab and therefore free access to it at any time during school's operating hours but also after hours and on Thursdays and Saturdays when school was closed. The professor and I became good friends and very often went out on Saturday mornings, either in town or to the nearest park or rural areas to shoot pictures of urban architecture or marvels of nature. Although the club had eight members, most of them were mainly interested in lab works after school hours rather than going out for photo shoots. Consequently the outings were mostly carried out by the two of us which induced an atmosphere prone to confidences which would have never been brought up in a more crowded setting. I remember, once, telling him, while witnessing a picture progressively revealing itself in the revelator bath, that it reminded me of the discovery of Jesus' face which also progressively revealed itself to me on the "Santa Sidone" (the holy shroud) in Turin, Italy…

From this moment on, I was always heading to my long walks or bicycle runs with my camera around my neck, stopping and snapping whatever I saw worthwhile. When back at school, the development of my films and pictures was occupying most of my weekly leisure time. The marriage of photography and sightseeing, my two passions, was perfect and I loved it!

The definitive move to Clermont-Ferrand made me lament the loss of my friends. It was with them that I went to primary school; with them that I played soccer; with them (at age eighteen) that I passed the medical exam for the conscription to the mandatory French military service; with them that I had spent almost a year of my spare time organizing the annual "Fat Tuesday Carnival" to celebrate the promotion of our military class of 1965. I was already missing my priest, the trips across France both by foot and by bus. At times I felt that I was betraying myself, rejecting everything that I was, pulling the roots of my life from under my feet… It was a sad feeling. On the other hand I must admit that, after seven years of schooling in Clermont-Ferrand, I had made new friends with whom I was spending more time than with my old buddies in Les Martres-de-Veyre. When I moved from CHARRAS to E.E.T.M I joined the sport's team of A.S.M ("Association Sportive Michelin") and pushed myself hard in both activities of running on the tracks of stadium: "Marcel Michelin" and swimming at the A.S.M swimming pool. The swimming pool was the only one covered pool in the whole town of Clermont-Ferrand and strictly reserved for the personnel of the company and their families. I was selected three times to participate in field and track scholar championships and brought back home several trophies reflecting on my prowesses. I also passed the diploma of assistant life guard which gave me the occasion to spend full paid vacations on the beach for one month at a time for two summer times in a row, ironically in:"Boyardville" in the island of "Oleron" where I went to, at the age of ten, to my first and only summer camp of my life!

After all, Les Martres-de-Veyre and Clermont-Ferrand were just ten kilometers apart or a mere ten minutes by car during normal traffic. I promised to myself that I will always stay in touch with my village, my priest and my friends. For my parents, the main anchor to Les Martres-de-Veyre was the mausoleum they had built in the cemetery of the parish for my little sister Brigitte. The construction, made of pink granite, was of good test and very much in line with the style of the moment; but above all this construction was the property of the WNUK's family, the first piece of real estate they ever owned in France. On one occasion, when mother and I were cleaning the mausoleum and changing the water of the flowers, she confided to me that I was not the elder of the family. She said that I had an older brother named: "Andrew" who was still born in the refugee camp in Germany. Her story was that, at the liberation, she met a Polish speaking American soldier who fell in love with her and promised to take her to the U.S.A. as soon as his time was over. Unfortunately, less than a month before my brother was born he got shot and killed by a resistant Nazi sniper located on the rooftop of a building… To my mother, the choc was such that she lost the baby. In retrospect, this encounter could have been the closest possibility for me to be born in the USA and therefore eventually predestined to live in Singer Island… but that did not happen. It was a near miss but, nonetheless, a miss!

CHAPTER 7

ANNE-MARIE

Anne-Marie kept visiting in Les Martres-de-Veyre, pretending to follow up on the attribution of the Michelin town house, but my intuition was telling me that, beyond all the pleasure she had spending time with my mother, she was also interested in me. In one occasion I suggested that we should eventually go out for a ride cross country and have a pick-nick by the river. She accepted so wholeheartfully that my mother even suggested that we use the family car. And so we did, and many times afterwards… but never alone since my brother and sister were always with us after having begged my mother to let them go and pleaded with Anne-Marie to say: YES! Anyway, overtime the ties between her and us grew strong enough for her to invite the Wnuk's to meet her family. Her family was rich. Dad made his fortune in the wine business and the manufacturing of knives in the famous town of Thiers (where my sister was born) also known as the French capital of "coutellerie" (cutlery).

The knives made there, and exclusively there, were allowed to carry the name of the town on the blade as a mark of authenticity. At the time we met Anne-Marie, her parents were retired and lived in the outskirt of Clermont-Ferrand in the town of: "Romagnat". We also met her sister, who was physically disabled, and had dedicated her life to God, as a nun, in a convent nearby. Anne-Marie was living by herself in an apartment on the first floor of a four stories building own by her parents. Few months after we met, Anne-Marie's sister died from a heart attack which was linked to her infirmity. That death and the following burial brought the two families even closer than they were before. Actually we felt as being one family with the elders (her parents who procreated at a late age), the mature adults (my parents), the young adults (Anne-Marie, my sister and I) and my brother, the kid who was eleven years younger than me. One day, I learned from my sister, that she had overheard a conversation between the two mothers conspiring at getting Anne-Marie and I married. According to Anne-Marie's mother, I was the son in law she always dreamt for her daughter. I was flattered to hear that but the prospect of getting married was not on my agenda, at least not yet… On the other hand, Anne-Marie kept mentioning a group of friends she was hanging with, especially one boy, by the name of "Yves", who owned a "Renault 8 Gordini" which, at the time, was the most snobbish street's sport-car that all girls were swearing by! I was annoyed but also jealous that she had her attention distracted from me by that other guy. Every time I was harnessing myself to seduce her, she was reacting as if she knew exactly where I was heading to and always dismissed my attempts with a smile, a couple of disarming laughs and a kiss on the cheek. Conscious of the transparency of my intentions and because of my unwavering loyalty to my strategy and tactic as far as chasing girls, I returned the kiss, hugged her amicably back and promised she will always be my big sister... nothing more!

Eventually the move to Clermont-Ferrand arrived. Now I was living in town. No more train to go to school, a bicycle sufficed and the family car became more available during the week days, especially in the evenings to meet with my schoolmates, either in town or in its surroundings, to do our homework together. The house was modest but modern and comfortable. Since the house was equipped with a shower and a bathtub, this time the portable tub did make it to the new place but was decommissioned and reassigned as a vessel to collect rain water, in the garden. Due to that, as well, there were no more trips to the public showers either. In a blink of an eye the hygiene and comfort increased "100%"! Now, we all felt as having reached the mythical "middle class status" that my mother dreamt of for so long. Ironically, the garden attached to the house was enclosed with a white picket fence!

When I received my military papers to join the army, the school had to justify my student's status to delay incorporation. This was done three times in a row until I graduated. In the meantime, I applied for a substitute "civil service" that would have given me the opportunity to travel and teach more unfortunate children in third world countries. The deliverance of my near future diploma which would sanction the length and the expected successful outcome of my studies were qualifying me, in advance, for such an endeavor. Unfortunately none of my requests were accepted on the premise that there were no openings at the time of my applications. Anyway, the final military papers were ordering me to join the: "GT 513" -Transport Group # 513 - of the 11th parachutist division located in the town of "Auch" in the South West of France. Auch is the town of "Dartagnan" the captain of the musketeers made famous in the novel: "the three musketeers" written by French author:"Alexandre

Dumas". I left behind my familiar town of Clermont-Ferrand, my scared and worried mother drowning in her tears, and climbed the train in the direction of: "Terra Incognita" with a black and white photograph of Anne-Marie, made by myself, in my wallet; but she was not there. When the train began to move, I looked at my family waving me good bye and saw in my mother's eyes the same fear she wore when, eleven years earlier, I was departing from the same train station for a summer camp in the island of Oleron on the Atlantic…

My attempt to do a civil service instead of a military one was mainly motivated by the prospective to travel more than anything else. Although as a child of WWII, I was never favorable to war as a solution to any conflict between people. I did my military service as the U.S.'s war in Vietnam was raging, keeping in mind that the French already failed that war (called then: "war of Indochina" which was composed of current Vietnam, Laos and Cambodia) and which the Americans were waging there and now to stop the spread of communism shortly after the French left. The same French military, following the war of Indochina, also failed the war of Algeria (a North African French colony) which ended with the independence of Algeria in 1962 after eight years of a bloody conflict that my division and my regiment fought very bravely but (politically) unsuccessfully! These were the military institutions I was joining in my way to Auch… The sixteen months of military service that I had foreseen as boring, demeaning and a pure waste of time turn out to be one of the best times of my life. After the three months boot camp, which was a nerve breaker for many, was for me, the occasion to push myself to my true limits, even more than my former training in the swimming pool or on the stadium tracks' at ASM in Clermont-Ferrand. Actually I loved it for the narcosis like feeling after the effort! At the end of my boot camp

I graduated as a parachutist, number: 268882, and was ready to be deployed to war zones where France was involved. Since none of that happened, I enrolled in the military school for non-commissioned officers which, after two months made me a drill sergeant with all the perks attached to the title and the function. From that point on, I enjoyed the privilege of having my own room in the barracks and enough money to spent, in town, dressed in civilian clothes instead of the military uniform. The girls in town knew us dressed in uniform and had already made their choice of who they would pursue with their charms if, by chance, some of us would show later as civilians after duty hours. For these girls it meant mainly easy money to benefit from and a convenient private bed as deemed necessary. Needless to say that both the money and the bedroom were used and abused profusely!

During the three months' boot camp I received several letters from Anne-Marie but then less and less. When once I inquired why, I was informed by my mother that she was talking about getting engaged. That was confirmed by Anne-Marie herself in a long letter where she was justifying her decision but never mentioned myself as a possible alternative. Finally by the end of my time I received an invitation to her wedding. On the card, the first name of the groom was the one of the owner of the Renault 8 Gordini. I disregarded the invitation and the black and white picture of Anne-Marie ended, torn into pieces, in a trash can.

At the end of my military service I reported to the head of personnel at the Michelin headquarters in Clermont-Ferrand. Since my employment was secured before my departure to the service, the only formality left to complete, prior to the signing of my full time work contract, was a three months probation period, required by law, which gave employers a last chance to fire a pre-hired employee who was not meeting any longer the hiring expectations… without justification! In the meantime, my new boss (and my former school director at E.E.T.M.) offered me the job of my dream consisting in teaching the Company's employees enrolled in continuous education! To achieve this objective, I joined the training department of the human resources service for a five weeks training in teaching and pedagogical techniques. Upon completion of the training, I was ready to hit the classroom stage in front of a huge blackboard. This in house continuous education was a perk of the Company for its meritorious employees so that they could pass the necessary exams for an internal promotion in their jobs or prepare a move to some more rewarding positions. Since the Company was operational seven days a week, twenty four hours a day (in shifts) the training was open for business from 6:00 am to 9:00 pm. My fields of teaching consisted of: math, physics and machine design. My students' age was ranging from eighteen to fifty and their entry levels from 8th grade to associate of science in mechanical engineering. My schedule was made up of approximately twenty six hours of effective teaching at different levels and some twenty six hours of course preparation and homework correction per week. Officially, the legal working time, during my tenure, progressively decreased from 52 hours to 40 hours a week over 13 years.

Life was good! I lived with my parents. I was a bachelor and, outside my professional life, my main hobby (after hours) was to get with my two best buddies Gerard (surnamed "Tony") and Gilbert (a.k.a. "Cab", in short, derived from his last name). My surname was "San-A" after a sexy police superintendant popularized in the famous French detective novels: "Commissaire San-Antonio". We were spending time talking, drinking, smoking and chasing girls. By midnight or so we were parting to get some sleep for another workday the next morning. Our friendship was so strong that we solemnly swore that we will never break the bond which united us and, as a corollary that we will never marry. Women were plentiful and easy so there was no urgent need to secure a particular companion by means of matrimony. We were taking turns as far as using our cars to cruise around. Cab had a "Simca aronde, by Chrysler" Tony a "Peugeot 404" and me an "Opel record, by GM". Life was good indeed!

What should have happened finally did happen. The bond was broken… Tony married a country girl - Nathalie - he found, on a Sunday, herding her sheep back to the barn. Cab married a designer - Jeanine - working next to him in the machine design department of the Michelin Company. Suddenly I found myself alone, abandoned by my best friends!

CHAPTER 8

MEETING MY GIRL

For a while, I continued my nightly cruises from bar to bar, alone, until one day, I spotted three girls sitting in a corner of one of them, sipping white wine. The open bottle was still bathing in its ice cold bucket. I approached them with my glass of martini gin on hand and politely requested permission to sit with them. The answer was: YES. One was blond, the other brunet and the third dark black and curly haired. I sat next to the curly haired one. I learned that they were coming from a birthday party and, since it was only seven at night that, at least, a last glass for the road was on order before getting back home. The three of them introduced themselves as "Black Foot" or French nationals repatriated from the North African former colonies of Morocco, Algeria and Tunisia which wan their respective independences few years before. "Black Foot" reminded me of one of my teachers in elementary school. The one who used to call me: "golden helmet"… What a small world it was! The black curly haired was from Algeria whereas the other two were respectively from Morocco and Tunisia. They were in their early twenties. I was twenty two. I also learned that, as minors, they were not allowed by their parents to stay out passed eight o'clock at night and that they were just about to leave when I joined them. I found the idea of being at home no later than eight strange and ridiculous by French standards, but was explained that since they have lived in cultures, till the age of sixteen, predominantly Arab and Muslim, they were educated by their parents to abide by the local rules in order to preserve their dignity and the honor of their families. The commonly admitted decency required that, past eight, women having to go out should be accompanied by a male family member, being a husband, father, brother or cousin no matter what their age was. That aspect of the Arab culture was adopted by the French rulers and kept alive when they moved to France after the revolutionary wars of independence. After the last sip of wine, they all stood-up. We shook hands. On their way out they asked me if I would return to this bar, in which case they would be glad to see me again, any day, after five, at the end of their working day. They were all sales girls in the shoe department of a female apparatus mega store in Clermont-Ferrand. The blond girl had her driver's license and a car and they have been carpooling to work for the past two years.

 I did not go to the bar the following day but the day after. I did not want to show any urge to see them again, although the curly haired one began to occupy my thoughts more than I wished. She had the exotic look and accent of a girl "not from here". Something about her moved me in a way difficult to describe. She looked like a humane society's encaged puppy cat begging for adoption but at the same time, as a captive wild feline, unwilling to be tamed and ready to fight! What I did not know, at that time, was that this encounter would change my life, as I knew it, forever... When I entered the bar, I found her sitting at the same table where I met her for the first time, but she was alone. She said that her friends had to leave work earlier and that she was waiting for the 6:30pm commuter train to return home. The same train she used to ride each day before the carpooling deal. I ordered my favorite drink and offered to drive her home. She accepted joyfully and thanked me for my generosity along with her sincere excuses for disturbing my evening. I did not expect that kind of a discourse and tried to mitigate my "chivalrous" involvement. She asked that I leave her at the train station of her small town, in the outskirt of Clermont-Ferrand, so that no one suspected that she was riding with a man unknown to her neighborhood. I did as she asked and set another appointment at the bar for the next day. After a couple of meetings at the bar we decided to change the routine. I was to pick her up at her store after work and go for a ride to the countryside before returning to her home at around seven in the evening. That worked well especially during the warm days of late spring, summer and early autumn. We were lying on a cover in the middle of high grass and wild flowers. We were talking our brains out until exhaustion. She was plump, well rounded all over with the right "stuff" at the right places. Almost a perfect body if it was not for her constant regret of being a "petite" in size. She was dreaming about modeling or of becoming an actress or of being a famous artist... and of living by the tropical seas in a rustic cabana with the love of her life! Every time she was talking about her dreams, her eyes were tearing. One day she asked me about my dreams but I was not prone to tell her, as she was. I tried to be formal, realistic, practical, logic and all... It did not work. She wanted to know what was moving me, what was at the heart of my being. I knew, from that moment on, that pretence will not work with her and that only sincerity and honesty will win her to me. So I began to strip down all of my protections. I removed, layers by layers, the luster of the pride of who I thought I was in society and business. I spoke also about my family or more precisely: lack of, due to the choice my parents made to immigrate at the end of WW II. After a while, I figuratively stood in front of her "naked" and begging for her intimacy in order to hide my nakedness. She gave it to me more than I would have ever expected. She hugged me in tears with a strength that took my breath away. I said that I loved her and she said that she loved me too.

After about six months of dating she told me that it was time to meet her parents. That such a meeting, perhaps, would give us more freedom and time to be together on week-ends. I was not sure I was ready to go this far, that fast. Being with her was fine but becoming her semi-official boyfriend was another story. I was not in a hurry to leave my independent life style. Actually I felt even more independent since my friends were too busy courting their new conquests. When I was not with Chantal (the dark curly hair girl) I was still going to my favorite bars and night clubs to hunt for an easy flirt… My refusal to agree on a schedule for the meeting gave her cold feet and suddenly her beautiful smiley face turned angry and sad. I worked hard to explain that my week-ends were all booked since I was the appointed chauffeur of the family and that my mother was in charge of the week-ends' agenda… and the use of the family car. That meeting with her parents will not give us more time to be together because of this situation and that I could not do much about it since it was not my car and because I lived with my parents. She did not buy my story. She could hardly imagine how a twenty two year old guy, making his own money was so submissive to a mother who sounded to her like a "tyrant" to her own family. From that point on, no matter what I said, fell in deaf hears. She did not want to hear of me anymore and she asked me not to see her any longer. That evening I left her with a sense of relief and sorrow at the same time. Relief for being free again to go on with my libertine sexual life and sorrow for missing the opportunity to love her… all the way! From the beginning, I kind of knew that, with her, it would be marriage or nothing… and above all, marriage before consummation of sex. For a while, relief has won over sorrow; however the game of chasing girls became old and deception and boredom began to interfere with the short lived "quickies" I used to enjoy so much. One day I decided to see her again. I went back to the bar by the train station. She was there alone waiting for the 6:30pm commuter train to "Le Cendre", her town in the outskirt of Clermont-Ferrand. When she saw me, she stood up and walked towards me with a smile I had never seen before. It was a smile loaded with joy and gratitude but also regrets and pain. A smile begging for forgiveness and hope for a renewed strong relationship. We stood looking at each other for a while before we kissed a resounding: "HI", three times, on each other cheeks! We sat and, in a blink of an eye, two months went by as if it has never happened. I was happy… actually, very happy!

The meeting with her parents was scheduled for a Saturday evening at 6:00pm. Our schedule for that night was to go to a restaurant after the parental meeting, at 8:00 pm, with a return back home by midnight. Our schedule did not sit too well with her father. He told me, as if I did not know it already, that "well educated girls" in his country of origin did not go outside, after 8:00pm, unaccompanied by a member of the girl's family. That, if we left, right away, we would have plenty of time to have a bite and return home by 8:00! Not knowing the man any better and to please my "new love", I agreed to his proposal and we left after a quick before diner drink at their place. Needless to say that we stayed in the car, parked on the side of the road, killing time, since our reservation at the restaurant was for 8:00pm. Restaurants, in France, rarely operate before that time in the evening... as if my love's righteous father did not know it! When we returned to her home, it was well past 1:00am. She left me whispering a "good bye" so that nobody could eventually hear it and be awakened at such a late time at night... Yet she reminded me to be on time on Sunday morning, at 11:00am, since we decided to go for a picnic in the woods and grill an entire rabbit on a bone fire; one of my grilling specialties.

When I arrived at 11:00, she was there, in front of her house where a good dozen of men were working together on the finishing of a concrete fence. The subdivision she was living in was unfinished because of the high cost of construction and therefore all the neighbors, all from North Africa, decided to help each others with outdoor additions and landscaping in order to reduce the price. She was wearing a light pink mini dress and no make-up. When I approached her father to say hello, he ignored me pretending to be busy. Then I moved towards her, kissed her on the cheeks and motioned her to my car. We left with no further ceremony... When we arrived at my favorite place, at the end of a dirt road, a couple of miles away from the paved road, at the top of a hill, the view and the atmosphere were overwhelming. I spread a blanket on the grass in a clearing and started to unload the picnic. While she busied herself preparing the paper plates and plastic utensils, I brought a couple of stones and prepared the primitive barbeque I was good at building. Something I learned during my military service's surviving exercises. In the meantime I prepared two strong "manhattans" and we cheered to love and happiness while the rabbit was getting a "sun tan" that I was cooling down with a coat of homemade oily and spicy sauce. After a second drink, and with no warning, she pulled her dress over and threw it on the grass. She was bare! Naked! No underwear! Not a stitch! Nothing! My mind went blank. I did not know what to think or what to do… but the mental black-out did not last long. She turned around and I could see that her beautiful buttocks were wearing the marks of three belt lashes. The marks were red inside and bluish on the edges. Before I could say anything she grabbed her dress and put it back on. Then with tears in her eyes, she told me that her father beat her in order to punish her for disobeying his orders but also to learn how to behave to preserve his honor and the family's reputation. It was clear to me that I was responsible for this situation and that it was also a message from her father, to me, to make me understand that he, not me, was in charge… Blood was rushing to my head. My face must have been red with anger. I hugged her until I could utter a word, until the "white knight" in me had a plan in place to avenge her. I was outraged beyond description, speechless and feeling powerless in front of such a demonstration of injustice and brutality. When my inner self calmed down, I asked her if she would marry me. The silence which followed my demand was terrifying! I wondered if she would ever answer. After a while which seemed to have lasted an eternity, she did and she said: YES! Suddenly the sky was blue again; the hot summer sun was at its best to warm us after the icy cold moments we had just lived. We turned our attention to the rabbit and started to work on another drink in order to overcome our emotions and organize our thoughts. It was not quite 8:00pm when we arrived at her place. Her father was just coming out of the shower and her mother was busy preparing the diner. As we were going straight to the living room she asked her parents to follow us and sit for an important announcement. I did not let her speak any further and respectfully requested from him "the hand of his daughter", in the old fashion way, which he seemed to appreciate a lot! Here also, all of a sudden the air become more "respirable" and a smile covered the faces of both parents. Without hesitation he said: YES, followed by another unsolicited grateful: YES, from her mother. We sat for more than an hour and I was invited to stay for dinner. Not a world was said about the lashes. Up to that point, the "white knight" was gaining ground and I could see her soon out of her father's "donjon". On my way back home I was wondering how to announce my decision to my mother. At the same time I hoped that my posture at her father's place would stop the inhumane punishments he was inflicting to her, almost daily, for the sake of an imported culture which had no roots in France. Asking her for marriage was the first step towards freedom but it was not sufficient to take her out without going through more ritualistic moves. In order to make it "official", engagement was the next step. Obviously, at that point, I needed my parents' participation.

My mother fell into a depression. The thought that I would leave home was unbearable. She could not imagine what life could be without me... or more precisely without a "chauffeur", a "handyman" and an "administrative clerk" and whatever else she found me useful and good at! She would find herself alone with an aloof drunkard husband, a frivolous daughter and an adolescent son. She was about to lose her anchor and she knew that there was no need to fight it back. My determination was strong. She knew it and decided to play into my hands rather than seeing me gone for good. An appointment to meet my girl was set and at that moment all bets were out! As usual my mother, whose sense of hospitality was second to none, had the living room coffee table covered with sweets, cookies and soft drinks. Between the two women, it was "love at first sight". They embraced and kissed each other. Deep inside, I expected that to happen... and it did! An official date for the engagement was set, at that first meeting, and from that point on all was supposed to go… undisturbed. Chantal kept complaining about the Sundays that I was consecrating to my family but endured the inconvenience because of the engagement. Now she knew better who I was and at times regretted her harsh critics of me in the past. On engagement day which took place at her parent's house, there were family members, friends and neighbors. In a pure North African tradition, the lamb (mechoui) was barbecued in the backyard while kebabs were grilled and consumed along with before dinner drinks. The party lasted late at night. Finally, for her parents and mainly for her father, she was officially: "fiancée" and therefore he was no longer afraid of losing face, had she been seen with me in public, or had his honor impugned by undue gossips. For my mother it was a sad day. I was getting closer and closer to leaving her… alone.

I got quickly accustomed to my new status of: "fiancé". I was visiting her parent's house and she was spending time at mine's. Families were inviting each other and my mother even began to appreciate this extended family arrangement. Unfortunately, it did not last long. One day that I was visiting Chantal at her place, she called me to her bedroom and showed me again marks of belt lashes on her buttocks. This time it was not because of my transgression of her father's orders but because some "charitable" soul brought to his attention that she was flirting at work with a bunch of male workers who were all about her! Although I was silently outraged by the reason she gave me, but denied vehemently, I could not stand the tyrannical domestic brutality of her monster-father and the total lack of respect he was demonstrating toward her. She has left the shoe store several months before and was now working at an agency sub-contracting computing administrative support to small businesses. After three months of training in an "Information Systems" vocational center, she became the personal secretary of the manager of the agency. Due to her gorgeous looks and outgoing demeanor, she met the typical caricatured stereotype of the easy girl sleeping with the boss and partying with his associates. Although the idea of being cheated crossed my mind, that consideration came only second to the fact that the sadistic punishments of her pervert father were to stop in order to save her from physical and mental trauma. On that day, she confided to me that, back in Algeria, when she was nine or ten years old, her "virtuous" father's favorite punishment was to make her walk around the block, naked, to shame her either for being a bad girl or not having made the grades in school. That punishment lasted until a disgusted neighbor threatened to denounce him to the authorities for child abuse. On that day, since she was, by now, well passed twenty one, and therefore civically major, I decided to remove her from her father's presence. The plan was quite simple. I told her to pack her belongings discretely and be ready on the following morning to decamp from her parents house as soon as her father left for work. I took a day off as she did, and by 9:00am I parked in front of her house. She was ready, with a suite case and a bundle of loose cloths that we threw in the trunk of the car while her mother was begging her to reconsider… When we arrived at my mother's house, all was arranged for her to live with us for as long as it would take to protect her from the torture she was enduring at her former home. The evening before, I convinced my mother that Chantal was a martyr and that it was our duty to protect her. And she agreed. Violence and brutality, the hallmark of her youth, in Poland and in Germany, after the Nazi's invasion, was among the chief "villains" of civilization. She could not stand it and, in a minute, rejected all the good sentiments she had toward her father who was a con artist as far as portraying himself as a good and decent man who suffered the loss of everything he had when he was kicked out of Algeria… as was she, from Poland, but for totally different reasons. She did not want to have anything to do with him but regretted the loss of the warm kindness of her submissive and enslaved mother. My mother's rejection of him grew even bigger when one evening he came to see her and justified his abused punishments as the only things his daughter understood and deserved for disobeying him and that he did it, out of love, for her own good! While over hearing that from my bedroom, I ran onto him and chased him away into the street where he begged me to spare him from my knocks and kicks and, while running away, wished me good luck with my "slut".

Chantal was now part of our family. She shared my sister's bedroom and became a "Wnuk" at heart. At this moment, although at times haunted by the memories of my celibate libertine life, my fate was sealed. How could I not marry her? The ties and knots were so tightly knitted that I could not cut them out without spilling blood to death. At this point, marrying her was a matter of life and death. I chose life! The decision to move away from my mother's house was given to us when my sister, at the age of nineteen, announced that she was pregnant. She was not married but her boyfriend, a nice guy, promised to marry her as soon as he could afford and secure an apartment and take her with him. In the meantime my sister and the future baby were slated to stay at my mother's house… Due to short term foreseen space limitation, I resolved to go hunting for a dwelling myself and, after a few of unsuccessful attempts, found a beautiful studio on the 6th floor of a newly built apartment complex in the heart of Clermont-Ferrand. The name of the Residence was: "Residence Helios" which in Greek means: Residence of the Sun! We moved in with a full bedroom, a kitchen table, two chairs and a black and white TV set.

CHAPTER 9

FROM HELIOS TO HELIOPOLIS

After two months of enjoying our freedom and a new lifestyle as an unmarried couple, the time for planning our wedding arrived and occupied most of our conversations. As children of the cultural revolution of 1968, our motto was: "it is forbidden to forbid"; therefore living together before marriage, although not that common at that time yet, was not for us an impassable obstacle. On the other hand, having a traditional wedding was still part of our mores and traditions... although we did not truly believe in the binding power of the civil contract or the religious covenant as suggested by the religious and civil authorities of our time. In spite of that we moved ahead and tried to find a solution to a couple of issues which could have spoiled the show! Since I "kidnapped" Chantal from Her father, he was not talking to either us or my family. Not only he was not talking to me but he hated me for having scared the shit out of him, publically, when I ran behind him on the evening he qualified my fiancée: a slut! During that scene he lost all of his stature and begged me not to beat him. Since the kidnapping and according to Chantal's mother who kept calling us in secret, he was so humiliated that, for weeks, outside of work, he lived confined at home, avoiding contacts with the neighbors and declining all invitations. He was mortified by the fact that his lack of control over his own family had tarnished the luster he worked so hard to project and protect in the community. Due to her father withdrawal, we needed to find somebody to accompany her to the altar. She made the choice of an older man of the same age as her father. He was the spouse of a former shoe department supervisor who became Chantal's friend at the time she worked at the women apparel store. At a dinner at the older couple's place, the deal was sealed. The husband of Chantal's friend will accompany my future wife to the altar! The first obstacle was down. Two more were to go. The second one was the choice of a priest and a place to celebrate the religious ceremony. Not being "registered parishioners" in any parish in Clermont-Ferrand, I turned to my priest in Les Martres-de-Veyre for help. Although he was a traditionalist and did not support our decision to live together before marriage, he offered his help. The deal was completed at a fine dinner at my parents' place where he met Chantal who charmed him with her graceful and exotic manners. The priest made the necessary arrangements with his counterpart in the Parish of Clermont-Ferrand where we lived. He even offered to celebrate the wedding mass in his church of: "Saint-Genes des Carmes". The second obstacle was down. One more was to go. The third obstacle was of a different kind. It was about my father. The poor guy has had a "hit and run" car accident a year earlier, while riding his bicycle, and after 45 days in coma, he woke up back to life hemiplegic and brain damaged. His speech was impaired and blurred and he could barely walk. In spite of my insistence, he kept refusing to attend the wedding because of his handicap. Finally he accepted to make the effort to come when the priest convinced him that his presence was indispensable to make him and everybody at the wedding cheer after the mass with shots of "gnole"…

The date of April 3rd 1971 was set. It was a Saturday. All was arranged except for one more chore I had to do. It was to invite Chantal's parents to the wedding at the request of the priest. He recommended us to be charitable towards her father and to give him a chance to redeem himself, although due to his overblown pride, chances to seeing him at the wedding were very slim to non-existent. In thanksgiving to my priest, to the gentleman who accepted to accompany my wife to the altar and to my father, I reluctantly performed my duty by sending Chantal's parents a formal letter of invitation which she cosigned with me.

On the day of the wedding, the unexpected happened. Chantal's parents showed-up! He himself and his wife entered the lobby of Residence Helios where all guests gathered for an appetizer before leaving to the city hall where the civil ceremony, presided by the mayor, was to take place. He came to me, embarrassed, looking down and asked me if he could lead his daughter to the altar. I responded that it was for his daughter to decide. She coldly accepted and her "substitute father" retreated gracefully. The rest is history. Just looking at the joy reflected on Chantal's mother face was sufficient to forgive and forget…

We went on a two weeks honeymoon. The first leg of our trip took us to the Atlantic coast in the south west of France in the gulf of "Gascogne" where I used to spend summer vacations with my family. The second leg brought us to the foothills of the "Pyrenees" mountains where I did my military service. Finally, the third one, sent us to the Mediterranean cost from the gulf "du Lion" in the west to the "French Riviera" in the east, where she had family repatriated from Algeria, and where we spent two third of our time. A special event happened in the town of "Saint Tropez" (the summer French capital for the rich and famous and the hometown of actress: "Brigitte Bardot") and more precisely in one of its beaches, namely the beach of: "Pamplone". That beach, along with "Tahiti beach", is a nude beach and both were particularly popular in the late sixties and early seventies because of the previously mentioned cultural (and sexual) revolution of 1968. Going nude and practicing safe recreational sex was the thing to do (not necessarily at the same time or at the same place) in order to be "IN". In spite of our open-mindedness, doing "IT", i.e. going nude in public, was more difficult than we thought it was. Our minds were still partially jammed in the old traditions of Puritanism. Anyway, curiosity led us to the beach as being attracted by a magnet. After having parked the car and put on our swimsuits, we walked to the beach. We sat on a towel in a remote place on the beach which was already crowded in these late days of April. After few minutes of embarrassment I suggested that we should get nude, like everybody else, or leave the premises. Chantal teased me to dare. Without hesitation I removed my swimsuit at once and stared into her eyes while she was getting naked! All of a sudden a feeling of freedom and contentment overwhelmed us. From this moment on our lives underwent a fundamental change that is still present with us as I write these lines. We became practicing nudists and naturists at heart! On that first day of public nudity, I remember Chantal running to the water to cover up her naked body. After a moment in the water shyness gave way to enjoyment. When she emerged from her first bath, she rolled over in the sand until she was completely covered like a breaded Mediterranean fish ready to be baked in the Tropesian's sun. Then she stood in front of me and the others around displaying without complex her large and firm breast and her rebounded buttocks. This first exhibition was for her the genesis of our future erotic games which consisted, among others, to publish naked pictures of her in men's magazines. From that moment on, the excitement and pleasure she derived from exposing herself and being stared at by a great number of anonymous individuals made her behave as a libertine in the sphere of eroticism. It also made another feeling to emerge in me. It was the desire, not only to share the eroticism of her nudity with strangers, for their private enjoyment, but also to make her participate in the act of sexual excitement and consummation of sexual gratification with others. After hesitating to share my libidinous thoughts with her, I finally decided to go ahead and, to my surprise… she agreed to try if my own pleasure was enhanced at the idea of her fornicating with strangers! These thoughts began to germinate in our heads. That night, she was hot, and we made love madly. She admitted that going naked in public gave her an orgasm as soon as she hit the water!

Upon our return to Clermont-Ferrand we began to look at membershipping in nudist clubs. To our surprise, one of them was located almost next door to where we lived in the volcanic mountain of: "la Serre de Portelas". Its name was: "Club du soleil" (Club of the sun). We adhered to that one immediately and began to enjoy spending long week-ends in our newly purchased camping equipment. Having spent all of our vacation money on the honeymoon, in April, we could not afford to go on vacation in August, as most of all French workers do! Fortunately, a coworker and friend of Chantal, was generous enough to offer to spend the summer vacation month in her house that she occupied in the hamlet of: "Enval" in the municipality of Vic-le-comte, some fifteen kilometers from Clermont-Ferrand, heading south. That friend happened to be just married herself and was leaving also to her honeymoon for the entire month of August.

The once populated village of Enval was nearly abandoned. Most of the houses were unkempt or partially in ruins. Only nineteen people lived there which included a Spanish immigrant family composed of a couple and three children. Our friend's house, although big in size, had only one bedroom, a living space and kitchen combined in another room and a bath with shower only, all restored sufficiently for a decent occupancy. All the other rooms of the house were locked and inaccessible due to safety hazard. We moved in the day she moved out and settled to spend two weeks in the countryside away from the agitation of Clermont-Ferrand. The village, built on a cliff, resembled one of these typical villages of "Provence", in southern France, with houses seemingly piled one on the top of another. The whole cliff looked like one tall complex building with many mansions. This village was also known as: "le petit Nice" after the town of Nice on the French Riviera, for its micro climate which made the temperature always a couple of degrees warmer than the country around. I knew that village from the time I was scouting the region on my bicycle. It was not too far from Les Martres de Veyre and close to the river Allier. Enval means: in the valley, although the village itself was only partly in the valley and mainly on the north side of the valley. Due to its orientation east-west, it enjoyed the privilege of being sun shined from sunrise to sunset. A creek, a tributary of river Allier, was running at the bottom of the valley.

I was in love with Chantal and I was in love with the village. The cat we acquired few months earlier seemed to like this new environment also and she never made any attempt to run away from our friend's house. Somehow I knew that we were in for a good time... though I did not know yet how painful it will become on the long run!

We were spending time sunbathing naked on a secluded terrace away from anybody's sight, reading or just talking. Also we were fishing crawfish and trout in the creek or perches, breams and other small "fry fish" in the river Allier nearby. We liked to hike the country side for hours before returning to our nest, exhausted, ready for a couple of drinks which at times made us so stoned that we forgot to have a diner... fell in bed drunk, made love (or thought we did) and slept unconscious till the next daybreak! Additionally I put to test my painting skills which I had not used since I went to the military service. For several days, a couple of hours at a time, I went to the south side of the valley to paint the village in front of me. The simple act of running my brushes on the canvas was awakening in me emotions that I thought were dead for good and forever. As I was painting I remembered having been bribed by my schoolmates in primary school in exchange for my paintings. My favorite subjects were naked women sunbathing on sandy beaches bordered by coco trees and other palm trees, deer bucks in snow covered forests and icons of the Virgin Mary, the mother of Jesus. For my little friends I was a hero. The ultimate artist! For a handful of them, any homework that required designing or drafting or painting was systematically submitted to my attention, after school hours, for me to do it in their stead, so that they could score better grades the following day than what they could have earned on their own. The boys were straight forward proposing candies or marbles or even small change in exchange for my services. The girls were more "vicious". Some were using some tricks of their trade such as exhibiting an engaging smile loaded with promises or a begging pitiful face with sheepish eyes which, in both cases, made me do the work for free. The simple fact that my admirers were asking for my help, and not from others, made me feel superior and in control. Experiencing this sentiment was actually more important to me than any of their modest contribution to my artistic works. I had my following of "groupies" which made most of my male friends jealous. The feeling of superiority and control over others - meaning power - went beyond artistry and followed me in the field of seduction when I was leading my teenaged flirts, and later my adult affairs, to sexual submission. As a footnote about my paintings, and that outside of the school context, boys were mainly interested in naked women and deer bucks, as expected, and girls by icons of Mary and naked women… in that order, go figure!!!

Anyway, I enjoyed painting the village and after few years of interruption, the result was not bad at all. I still have the canvas hanging in my study in Singer Island. At the time I did it, I would have never imagined that it would, one day, end up in the "Garden of Eden".

As curious as I was, I decided to explore the abandoned village. I headed first to seemingly blind holes in the rock which turned out to be openings for windows and doors giving light to caverns hidden in the cliff. To my surprise, almost all the dwellings built against the cliff consisted either entirely of caverns with openings to the outside or made of real houses sitting on terraces on the cliff and hiding a cavern behind. One of these troglodyte houses, with a panel for sale covered by wild bushes, was right in the middle of the cliff and, for that matter, the village, and was running from a paved street at the bottom to a dirt road at the top covering, in height, the equivalent of a six stories building. One of the two caves behind the dilapidated house was twenty feet high and the adjacent one was large enough to house a typical Florida (lagoon style) swimming pool. My imagination was running wild. I saw the potential for a great unusual and original home that nobody else would have ever had. A perfect nest for our newly married couple...

When I reported my findings to Chantal, she was excited by my own excitement. After having her to climb up a narrow trail to visit the house on the cliff, we both agreed that, if we could afford it, it would certainly be the ideal place to live out our dream of naturism in perfect harmony in the bosom of mother earth.

These special vacations saw us returning to Clermont-Ferrand brewing with just one project in mind: our future house in Enval. To make a long story short, let's just say that I found the financing to buy "the ruin", as my mother put it and enough money left over to begin renovation. In the meantime Michael, our son, was born on the 10th of November 1972 and we moved from the studio to a three bedroom apartment in the same residential complex of "Residence Helios". Chantal began to attend the Art University of Clermont-Ferrand, at walking distance from our place, and rejoiced between mothering our baby and studying art part time. She specialized and graduated in pottery, sculpture and painting. The frequentation of the art academy provided a lot of new friends from the "democratic social liberal" side of the political spectrum. The traditional liberalism of teaching institutions, exacerbated by the cultural revolution of 1968, made life, sex and love front and center of our thinking, discussions and decision making processes. The pre-revolution taboos were all dead and again the slogan: "it is forbidden to forbid" and: "if it feels good, do it" were running wild in our lifestyle. While Chantal was attending the art academy I enrolled in a grass-root political movement called: "Perspectives et Realite" (Perspectives and Reality) founded by hopeful finance minister: "Valerie Giscard d'Estaing" in preparation to his bid for the French presidency of 1974. Giscard, in short, as everybody called him, was an independent moderate conservative "center right wing" politician and the official representative of the "Gaullist" ideology. As an admirer of "General de Gaulle", a former two terms French president and Hero of World War Two, my affiliation with Giscard was more than natural. It is also worth to mention that Giscard was young, brilliant and a strong supporter of the 1968 revolution; specially as far as bringing down the alienating taboos of the past related to the French obsolete Puritanism and stringent conservatism. For a descent of the (officially) deceased nobility whose some members were killed during the 1789 French revolution, it was an act of courage and independence that the people appreciated and it showed in his election to the presidency. Here also we met new friends with very open minded backgrounds and started a great family of intellectuals and artists. Life was busy and exciting…

Our friends from the naturist club recommended that we go spend time on: "Ile du Levant" (the island of the rising sun) which, at that time, was considered as the "Mecca" of naturism in the Mediterranean Sea right off the coast of the French Riviera. We did it in 1973 and pitched our tent in the private garden of a local land owner. We shared the garden with her niece who was also camping there for the summer. Michael was nine months old and discovered naturism at that early age as a natural way of life. His innocent mind never questioned the validity of living naked among nude people. Needless to say that he was the talk of the town and was adored by whoever came close to him. The name of the town was: "Heliopolis" meaning "the town of the sun" in Greek. We kept coming four times during the following six years and made our landlord's garden our month of August summer home. We were dreaming about buying a piece of the island to make it our own summer house. Needless to say that dreams were cheap but the real estate unaffordable for our means at that time… and besides, the house of Enval was swallowing all the savings we could have made!

THE INVISIBLE HAND

Sea, sand, sun (and sex), as went a French popular song in the mid-seventies, were the ingredients which filled our days at "Ile du Levant".

Sea in the morning, when we were free diving for sea-urchins, in order to eat them, as an appetizer, with the before lunch drinks, usually white wine or rose. Our diving group was composed of a dozen of friends which included two foreigners: "Rose-Marie", an American girl from Philadelphia who, for the time being, decided to live in Nice and another from Switzerland who was camping with her teenage son. We also had a surgeon from Paris, his wife and two daughters. All the others were locals from the nearby French Riviera including a gay couple. Sea also in the afternoon, after a nap, to spear-gun fishes and octopuses used in the preparation of the traditional southern French: "bouillabaisse", a heavy soup loaded with seafood and fish. Sea, finally, in the evening, when, as in the morning, we were paddle boating, back and forth, in our inflatable boat from the harbor of Heliopolis to the beach, half a mile away. The beach was adjacent to a submarine military base which covered three fifth of the island. The rest of the island, including the beach was privately own and incorporated into an owners' association named: "ADIL" standing for "les Amis De l'Ile du Levant" (the friends of the island of the Rising Sun) which membership and ownership required the practice of nudity and the promotion of naturism.

Sand, exclusively at a place called: "La Pinede", consisting of the sandy beach mentioned earlier, surrounded by a forest of pine trees. Because the island itself is a mountain rock in the sea it makes this sandy spot very valuable for naturists in the whole non-military Heliopolis estate.

Sun, of course, always present, was the reason for the season… and sex!

Sex, was in the air at all times, not only because of the sex appeal and attractiveness of some well endowed nude bodies but because of the games we were playing in the buff. Taking sexy glamour pictures or super 8 movies, at the hard to access secluded place called: "la piscine" (the swimming pool) was one of them. And a heavily sex loaded one since the women, but also men, who volunteered to pose were not ashamed to submit to the requests of the horny group of photographers, male and female, and did not hesitate to go beyond their wildest desire in simulating embraces. Some simulations were ending up in hilarious orgasms, irrepressible premature ejaculation or in welcomed uncontrolled joyful copulation thanks to Rosemary, the American girl, a porn-starlet, who was often directing the erotic poses. As a footnote I would like to add that Rosemary played in a full-length pornographic film that we watched in a specialized movie theater during one of her multiple visits in Clermont-Ferrand. Another game was body painting… and more pictures taking during the process. If some pictures taken were for personal consumption most of the others would find their way to erotic or pornographic magazines which, for all who posed and exhibited themselves, made the game of picture taking so exciting. Although these happenings were not every day events, not to say… rare and exceptional, they always made a lasting impression in my mind when they occurred! Sunbathing, swimming to cool the heat of the sun, more sunbathing and lingering conversation until sundown was the core of most time spent during the day. At night, in hotels' bars and night clubs, flirting was in order! Swapping partners was also very much the thing to do if one wanted to be "IN"; although swapping was not a thing we shared with our nudist friends when we were going out together. Chantal and I, however, used to engage in the game of flirtation with strangers with no hesitation since we were looking for such an opportunity from back when we disrobed on the beach of Pamplone in Saint Tropez. We both knew the rules. Flirtation was seen as a performing art of seduction, aimed at, and leading to a sexual gratification, whenever achievable, and only that! No feelings of "true love" were allowed. The sublimation of eroticism to ensure a supreme orgasm exacerbated by the simple fact of achieving it, with a perfect stranger, outside the boundaries of conventional intercourse, was the goal. As consenting partners in the game, we were going ahead with no mental blockages and always hoping for a successful satisfactory completion of the lustful act.

PART II

CHAPTER 10

A TICKET TO AMERICA

The six first years of our marriage were lived in the fast lane. Besides our main activities, for me at work, at the political club or on the construction site of Enval - as we referred to the house we were building there - and for her at the art school, in the beginning, and later as a professional artist in her own shop, we were busy scheduling parties for the week-ends either with our family, friends or ourselves alone!

Family parties were fun in the beginning, especially shortly after the wedding, but quickly became old since a sort of routine settled down and the reunions were felt, at times, more of a burden or an obligation than a recreation. We were going in turn from one family member to another until the circle was closed and started all over again. Since we were not the only ones fatigued with this kind of arrangement we, along with others, progressively broke the circle of boredom and decided to meet occasionally, not on a formal basis but on a more casual and joyful one! Friends of our families became our friends as well. As the "clan" was growing out of proportion, it was time to stop the process of constant weekly invitation and preserve a space for privacy that we did cherish before the wedding, and lost for a while, in order to please everybody.

Scheduling private home parties for us two alone was more enjoyable than we would have ever expected. The parties were always beginning with a long stay in bed, in the morning, followed by a late brunch with coffee and "bloody Maries" and then there were games. The games always had a sexual connotation and were played for money or for sexual arousal. The looser had the choice to either put $5 in a box or submit to a bet which involved some sort of risky indecent exposure! After the games came more drinking and smoking and a lot of talking before making love, anywhere… but in bed! Eventually a diner was to conclude the day. During the hot days of summer we were going outside for a picnic in the country. The motivation was the same with the same outcome… It was during one of these outings that Chantal and I decided to take erotic pictures and post them, for the first time, in men's magazines. Although Chantal was the only one modeling in the nude or in erotic outfits, she was also suggesting poses. For that, she was, at the same time, the model and the picture director imitating in that our friend Rose-Marie from Philadelphia. My contribution was to apply my skills, as a technician and a photographer, to optimize my camera's features and to catch the best angle for the greatest erotic impact. Overtime we made four submissions. All of them were accepted with follow-up layouts done by the magazines' professionals. Needless to say that the layouts on the glossy pages of the magazines would have damned more than one saint! Knowing that thousands of eyes were looking at her and lusting over her was another motivation to keep on going and enjoying sex as never before!

We also became very much involved scheduling parties with friends alone and, along the way, developed special friendships with couples seeming to be open to swapping. The clues which led to acknowledge and to materialize the exchange were very subtle but evident for like-minded people. When a tacit agreement was reached, we then made sure that only one couple was involved at a time. No matter what we did, we made sure that no exclusivity or hidden jealousy was preventing couples to swap at will, going back and forth from one partner to another, or even to make love in a threesome or foursome fashion. Heterosexuality happened to be the rule between men but homosexuality took place once between Chantal and another girl, to the delight of the men watching them touching each other or playing with sex toys. We had up to four couples involved with us, separately, which did not know the others. At times, scheduling was difficult since the others believed that we were their sole swapping partners… Anyway the more the merrier!

Swapping or swinging became just another normal activity and, as expected the promiscuity inherent to such an activity led to cheating. Not as defined conventionally but in a way similar to having an affair revealed to the married partner and pursued with her or his consent. It was practiced whenever opportunities arose either with mutual friends of ours or even complete strangers, similarly to when we were practicing separate flirtation in Ile du Levant, which then, was limited to few weeks, during summer time, in order to sharpen our sexual desires for the rest of the year! When the cheating began, although acknowledged as a break of our rules, no reproaches were made either way since freedom to please ourselves and open-mindedness were the goal and philosophy of our sexual lives! "Adultery" was not part of our vocabulary either since lusting over some attractive other was part of the new normal for the "newly liberated sexual being of the sixties". These words and concepts were part of the vocabulary of the ancient times and did not apply to our lifestyle. Neither did apply descriptors like "pervert" or "depraved" which were used to judge the natural tendencies of the human race to copulate for procreation but essentially for recreational sex outside the sphere of self-preservation. This sexual freedom removed all the stress linked to our natural needs and desires that both of us agreed to respect and satisfy with gratitude to the willing and obliging partner! Actually that was all what naturism was about: living life naturally with no frustrating or exalting taboos. And let's make no mistake about the swinging lifestyle: it had its timing and the right circumstances for execution under control. It was only when the moment was right and the partners were ready… that the exchange began. It needs also to be said that the frequency and the scope of the games represented a small part of our lives… although the better part of it!

We were in the finishing stages of Enval, and probably a couple of months away from moving in, when my boss called me and asked if I would consider going to the USA for a temporary assignment. Michelin was expanding worldwide and among other things decided to return to the USA where World War I ended, for a while, its operation on the North American continent in Milton, New Jersey. I knew that a "rubber plant" was being built in Anderson and that a "tire plant", along with the American headquarters, were under construction in Greenville, both in the state of South Carolina, but never imagined that I could be of any use for the expansion, in my current capacity as a technical instructor who, by the way, spoke English. Actually my boss needed just that. He wanted me to go there to hire new employees, freshly graduated from technical schools and colleges, and train them so that they could apply and effectively utilize their newly acquired knowledge and skills in the factory positions they were destined to. This proposal left me speechless! We have been dreaming, since Chantal and I met, to go abroad... and now the dream came true. I did not know how decisive my answer was when I said: YES! My assignment was for no more than six months, due to immigration and taxation US regulations. Chantal was scheduled to join me for one month, in the middle of my stay. Our son Michael, who was already spending a great deal of time (mainly during week-ends) with his grandparents from both sides, was almost happy to see us go in order to spend even more time with them...

1977 was the year when Elvis Presley died and a definitive marker in our lives. During these six months, and more precisely when Chantal was with me, over long week-ends and few days off, we have visited Graceland in Memphis-Tennessee, Disney World in Orlando-Florida, Daytona Beach nearby and the Kennedy Space Center in between, the Cherokee Indian reservation in the Appalachian Smoky mountains of North Carolina, Atlanta-Georgia and Stone Mountain, the Blue Ridge scenic route 11, Charleston and Myrtle beach in South Carolina! The names were magic. With our preconceived and incomplete knowledge of the USA, what we saw and what we lived went beyond our expectations. Even the way the houses were designed and built (wooden structure), with plenty of space and top notch appliances, integrated kitchens and air conditioning was amazing for us "French". We were absorbing and cherishing our discoveries as if we would never see them again. Beside the well built subdivisions sitting in perfectly groomed landscapes and manicured lawns, we dared to visit the less privileged sections of Greenville downtown which, at the time, were unkempt, mostly deserted and for some, squatted by the homeless and the disenfranchised at the exclusion of the residential historic preservation areas, in the outskirt of downtown, at a walking distance, where were the homes of the rich and famous… There, the architecture of the houses (Victorian, Tudor, French, Dutch, Colonial and others), the tall pecan trees and oaks in the backyards and colorful azalea bushes, dogwoods and magnolia trees in the front yards transported us to the time of "gone with the wind". Discovering America from the "Deep South" angle was also a challenge since most of the stereotypes of the American image, as seen from Europe… were not there! We were in "Redneck" country and the "Buckle of the Bible Belt". There was still an active Ku-Klux-Klan chapter in nearby Spartanburg and we discovered that "Bob Jones University" - a white conservative extremist Baptist church and school - was ruling the society of upstate South Carolina as well as the entire "Bible belt" which Bob Jones was the "buckle". At the university, black and white mingling was tolerated but not encouraged and interracial wedding strictly forbidden. The "Blue law", consisting of selling no liquors on Sundays, was in effect in Greenville County although consumption of booze in vehicle was permitted at all times. By contrast, guns were clearly visible on pick-up trucks' racks and kinky sex was practiced widely… underground. That America was not glamorized abroad as much as Manhattan in New-York with its skyscrapers or California with its Hippies in San Francisco or Orlando with Disneyworld or Las Vegas in Nevada with its casinos and lustful lifestyle or Miami with its "vice" or Texas with its TV series: "Dallas". Although Greenville S.C. was once called the "textile capital of the world", what was left over of it, after the ending of slavery, was a town cluttered with closed textile mills in the outskirt and abandoned downtown buildings such as the "Woolworth" store and the "Poinsett" hotel, which, at one point in time, were the landmarks of the greatness of the South. From abroad we knew that Washington and Lafayette wan the "the Revolutionary War" or the war of independence from the British ruler, but did not know that the whole thing started in the French Huguenot town of Charleston. Those Huguenots who fled from France under Catholic persecution were, with the British Protestants, the co-founders of the town. We learned also that in Charleston, as in neighboring Atlanta, were written the saddest pages of the "North and South" secession war which marked the demise of the South. Even the "Cherokee" Indians of Appalachia did not have much in common with the Indians of my childhood's cartoons. There were no teepees anywhere and there were no traces of the conquest of the west as depicted and glorified in "Western" movies. Anyway, the surprise fueled our curiosity to discover and learn more about that unknown and unpublicized America which, for us, was about to become part of France thanks to the implantation of Michelin in Greenville SC. Actually, drawing a parallel between The USA at large and South-Carolina was pretty much like comparing Clermont-Ferrand to Paris. The former almost unknown for many but mainly known by the users of Michelin tires for housing "the manufacturer of the best tire at the best price" and the latter as the city of lights and the talk of the world! This being said, I prefer Clermont to Paris because of the volcanoes and of "Vercingetorix", the king of the Celtic-Gaul who defeated Cesar in 52 BC... at "Gergovie" (which is the name of a high plateau dominating Clermont and was Vercingetorix' capital) as popularized through the movie: "Druids", and for the pope Urbain II who preached the first crusade from "place de la Victoire", facing the 1000 years cathedral, and for "Pascal" who invented the first calculator, and because... I am a little bit of a chauvinist! But I digress.

For the time Chantal was with me, we took advantage of being together in a foreign environment to immortalize our presence abroad by taking tons of pictures and super 8 movies. One would imagine that, with our state of mind and her exhibitionistic tendencies, that some of them would be erotically oriented... so yes, they were! For these pictures, in particular, I had chosen a background that unmistakably showed that they were taken in the USA. Similarly, when we went to Algeria, twice, to defuse the nostalgia Chantal was still cultivating after her repatriation to France. There we went on a photo shooting spree which allowed us to present for publication erotic and exotic pictures of her in the sandy dunes of Ouargla and the bazaar and oasis of Gardahia in the Sahara desert.

Now, after several years of playing with sex and enjoying it so much, we became the promoters of and the partakers in our own erotic games either together alone or with others. Erotic Naturism (Eroticism) was, so to speak, our new religion and Eros our God. And what an enjoyable religion it was, innocently unencumbered, as compared to the guilt-ridden irksome Catholicism, which we continued to adhere to, more by tradition than conviction, and which keeps preaching that SEX is SIN and SIN is SEX, period... no more explanation needed! How does that square with "sexual purity" preached in the more liberal Christian churches? In truth, sexual purity, for us, was a combination of lust and love. Lust as the ultimate goal and the cement of our romantic relationship and love as the emotional complicity we shared in the honesty and transparency of our intentions and actions. Nothing was hidden from one another and we were never ashamed of our sexual activities. She knew me well and I her too. Retrospectively, I must admit that the lifestyle of our choice greatly contributed to our faithfulness and tenderness towards each other in a way that a typical marriage would have never achieved. The commandment of our "sensual erotic religion", which kept us in check, was: "it is good if it feels good and bad if it feels bad!"

The memorable experience of living and working in America gave way to the harsh reality upon our return. Actual life in France was not the dream life we had for a while, mixing work and play on a permanent basis. Most of the time it was: work, and occasionally: play. At the following summer vacation we skipped: Ile du Levant and went on a five weeks trip to Great Britain in hope to resurrect our time in the USA… if by no other means but the language… no matter how broken it was! We drove our own camper and designed our itinerary so that we could park every night in a nudist camp. They were many across the country from England to Scotland and everywhere in between. We had a wonderful time, especially on a small island called "Inch marine" on the "Loch Lomond" in Scotland. Overtime I noticed that my American English became slightly tinted by the British accent which, as everybody knows, is quite different from the American one and more precisely from the one of South Carolina.

After returning to Clermont-Ferrand, I met with my boss and expressed my desire to work for the Company abroad. He promised to consider my request and to answer it if any opportunity arises. When he called me in his office, I was miles away from imagining what I heard. He explained that the Company was looking to expand in the Middle East. More precisely in Egypt, in the town of "Alexandria" in the outskirt of the capital: "Cairo". Although the commercial, administrative and, unfortunately, political arrangements were still a couple of years from completion, some preliminary groundwork was already in progress such as the purchase of the land where the manufacturing plant and the headquarters would be built as well as the lease of a building, in town, where the future employees would be trained prior to their assignment. In the meantime this facility was destined to be used as a technical school where teenagers, as of the age of sixteen, would receive a technical formation to become professional in machine design and which would, eventually, land them a job with the Company at the time of operation. I was offered to become, at first, the director of the school before taking over the management of the training center. I was assigned, along with twelve other members in my team, to begin studying the Arabic language and to prepare for a departure in about a year from that moment… I was astonished by the proposal to work abroad but also by the promotion which came along with it. At the age of thirty one I had it almost made! When I announced that to Chantal, on the evening of that day, she could not believe it either. The Middle East was even better than America because it was geographically closer to her native Algeria, in North Africa, and was very similar culturally. After several months of intense studying of the language, I became (almost) fluent and spoke only in Arabic with my professor and also new friend. As the departure time drew near, but was several times postponed, the fear that things were not going well took roots in our mind. Confirmation of it happened when the cancellation of the Egyptian project was communicated laconically by the spokesman of the Company who mentioned, in passing, as I understood it, that political incompatibilities, having to do with the managing partners' voting rights, were the cause of the break-up. Chantal and I were devastated. For more than a year, our thoughts and conversations were all but about Egypt. She even designed a belly dancer outfit that she had already worn a couple of times at parties while performing dances that she learnt with the wife of my Arabic professor. What a blow! All of that for nothing! Anyway, life went on. I was re-assigned to go to a nine months training that, at the end would have made me a "cadre" which, in the American lingo, means: "senior manager". That was without counting with the "Invisible Hand" which, half way before completion of the training had my head instructor and my former boss call me for a meeting. What they had to say was another surprise. This time, Michelin was expanding in the USA, and, as back in 1977, I was needed to repeat in "Austin" Texas, what I did in Greenville S.C. The main difference was that, at that time, I was assigned as the training manager for the entire new operation which was to cover the needs in training for the manufacturing units of Austin, Midland and San Antonio. We were in January of 1980 and, according to a timeline agreed upon by my boss and myself, a departure time for the whole family was scheduled for mid-April. In the meantime I was to undergo a total immersion in the English language, in England, first in the University of Canterbury for three weeks followed by a five weeks stay at the Institute for English studies: "Linguarama" in Winchester.

When we left France for the United States we left behind family and friends; Michael's school and neighborhood, where at age seven, he already had his network of friends and activities he liked to participate in, in and out of school and home; Chantal's well established business as a potter and sculptor... and the house of Enval. The assignment was for three years. We knew what we were leaving but still very little of what was ahead of us. Chantal and I were still under the spell of a country new to us and were seeing ourselves more as vacationers than residents.

We arrived in Greenville, at first, from where we were to move to Austin shortly after. The land for the manufacturing facilities in Texas was already purchased and the building acquired to dwell the training center in Austin was under renovation. While waiting for an imminent departure, we lived in rentals in Greenville. Michael went to the French School sponsored by Michelin and Chantal attended the community college where she began to learn English. As for me, I prepared with my team of four to move to Texas. The preparation consisted essentially to put together the courses being taught, to select and procure the pedagogical aides needed to facilitate the teaching process and to work out the class schedules so that each of us had a fair share of lecture time, workshop attendance and administrative chores. After a month or so, we were informed that the Texan project will be delayed and that the hiring and training of the future employees will begin in Greenville until any move is envisioned. So it was, and after four months with no change in sight, most of the newly trained employees accepted to be re-routed to Lexington, close by Columbia, the capital of South Carolina where a new tire plant was just beginning its operation and was in need of qualified personnel as soon as possible. After a year, it became clear that the expansion in Texas will never happen... and it was officially declared as such shortly after! So much for Texas! My assignment was maintained and the remaining of my time spent in retraining salaried employees in need of additional knowledge in their current jobs or for promotional purposes. Feeling that our American adventure was heading to an end, we decided to take a five weeks cross country vacation which took us from the east to the west coasts and from the north to the south ends of North America. In the US, the bench marks of the trip included the Petrified forest, the Painted desert, the Grand canyon, Las Vegas, the Death valley, Los Angeles, Disneyland, Hollywood, San Francisco, the Sequoia and Yosemite national parks. In Mexico, we travelled from El Paso to Chihuahua to Durango to Mazatlan to Guadalajara to Mexico to Monterey, to Nuevo Laredo...

The return to France was nearing and, one more time the sadness invaded our household.

CHAPTER 11

THE INVISIBLE HAND

Finally when all hope of staying in the USA was exhausted, the Invisible Hand played its joker. I received a phone call from the president of the US operations to meet with him in order to discuss a job proposition. Although I knew him from France, as a friend of my boss, and through many business meetings in the US, I felt uneasy when I entered his office. He was friendly and cordial, as usual, but his face was somber and his speech awkward. The job he was in need of has already been turned down by a couple of potential candidates and, as he told me later, he was not expecting any more success with me. The job was a high profile, very visible one, which could have made me the perfect "scapegoat" and an easy excuse, for higher ups, in case of failure on their part. Not only the job required a solid technical background but also a good knowledge of manufacturing processes and also shrewd political skills and a natural sense of self preservation to survive the corporate American culture. After a long description of the job, which included numerous embarrassing repetitions, I accepted. The president remained silent for a while then asked again if I was sure I can handle the job. Without hesitation, I said: YES! A conditional "yes" which demanded that I get an exposure to all the trades associated with that job and to meet and acquaint with all the people, in France and in the US, having a stake in my future dealings with them. The condition was agreed upon and a contract, including my demands, was drafted by the head of human resources which, then, after review, was confirmed and made official in the next following days. To my surprise, when I was called again to sign the contract, was also included the condition that I would resign my French expatriate status and become an American employee upon the issuance, by the INS (Immigration and Naturalization Service) of my permanent residency in the US (Green Card) which, in the meantime would have been applied for and sponsored by the Company. I did remember the President alluding to a long term commitment but did not remember him mentioning a "Green Card" as part of the deal. Anyway I accepted this condition as an uneventful necessity, not realizing yet that I was signing my French life away. There again, I explained to Chantal and Michael that we needed to prepare for a brief return to France, for a year, including ten months of training and two months of vacation, one before and the other after the training period. We would live in our house of Enval, which was finished and furnished… as if we were to return after another professional stay abroad, except that this time there will be no coming back!

Entering the house, on a hot summer day of 1982, was like inhaling a breath of fresh air, literally and figuratively. Literally because the main entrance was communicating with the living quarters located in the main caves where the temperature was averaging seventy degrees Fahrenheit, year round, when the temperature outside was in the mid nineties in the summer and freezing in winter. Figuratively too because of the refreshing thought of impregnating the house again with our lives, even for just a year, which ending, at that moment, was so far away that it seemed it would never happen… I was happy and sad at the same time. Chantal was sad also for not being in America as well as Michael who knew that he would spend his next scholar year in a boarding school with visits to home on week-ends only. The decision to send Michael in a boarding school had two purposes. One was to teach him independence and the second to teach him discipline which he was lacking at home and in the regular schools he has attended so far. In other words we were hoping that "others" would be more successful in the area of parenting that we have abdicated, almost since his birth. Needless to say that his grandparents, on both sides, were not blameless in spoiling the wonder kid who he was! Michael was beautiful as a baby and then as a child, very lovable, smart and outgoing. In every school he went to, he was surrounded with groupies who adored him but which cruel favorite game was to entice him into some "crazy" action or behavior in which he would be caught and punished for by the teachers. Michael knew the end result of the game but kept playing it in order to retain his followers' attention! My visits to the principals were innumerable… yet, after a soft talk to reprimand him, he knew he would be forgiven and therefore tacitly allowed to start all over again the following days. I never had the heart to punish him physically since I never had to undergo such a humiliating treatment myself, neither was his mother who was the victim of a tyrannical father.

The training for my new job was great! Although I knew the Company's business quite well, in general, getting into the nitty-gritty knowledge of the tasks, their execution and management was a completely different experience. When I left Clermont, back to the US, I was under the impression that I had a legion of people backing me up, people whom I knew as persons and as "wells of knowledge" I could count on. In my area of expertise, I became the "liaison" between France and the US, the point of contact through whom all my specialty questions will be channeled to. I was proud of my performance and even more proud of the training report issued by the French Head of human resources. I was on my way to play my role in "team USA".

In the meantime we restarted visiting and inviting family and friends. True friends responded: present! Not so true friends excused themselves on the pretext of business. Some family members were happy for us, others started to show jealousy and even some blamed us for abandoning them. As for the swingers of parties long gone, while trying to reignite the erotic flames of the past, they looked surprised that we still remembered that… and them! We had to realize that our choice to live in the US made us pariahs and that our relation with our French connections, no matter how frequent, will never be the same.

A month or so before leaving Enval, we made arrangements to move our belongings to the US and, to the delight of my sister and brother in law, we rented them the house and helped them to move in. For a month or so the whole Wnuk's family became guests in their own house.

Upon our return to the US we rented a furnished house in the subdivision of: "Del Norte", in the surroundings of Greenville, and recuperated our two cars and few personal belongings from the storage. Less than six months after, we purchased a four thousand square foot, two stories house, built in 1910, in one of the historic preservation areas of Greenville. The house was listed in the National Register of Historic Places. At the same time we removed Michael from the French Michelin School and put him in a bilingual program at: "Holly Elementary School". At the same time, Chantal registered again at: "Greenville Tech.": the local Community College, to further improve her English. Since she could not work, because of restrictions by the INS, prior to the issuance of the Green Card, she decided to learn welding, in the vocational section of the college, in preparation to her future job as a metal sculptor. This is where she met Clyde, the head of the vocational department of Greenville Tech and part time welding instructor. Clyde, a veteran of the Vietnam War, married with a Vietnamese woman and father of two girls was a typical Southern gentleman with a heavy southern accent (the Drawl). With me he was polite and respectful. With my wife, he was fascinated by her beauty and committed to do all he could to help her with her broken English as well as her desire to become a metal sculptor… In the meantime, he introduced her to the Youth Correctional Center, in Simpsonville, in the outskirt of Greenville, where she volunteered to teach Art to the inmates.

After settling on Earle Street, I began to draw plans to restore the house and improve the landscaping of the front and back yards overgrown with pecan trees, dogwoods, magnolia trees, cedars, oaks, azaleas and jasmine… This time was one of the busiest of my life. On one hand I was taking care of my new job, working sometimes up to sixty hours a week, including week-ends, and on the other hand supervising home improvements, following on Michael's progress in his bilingual program and sharing Chantal's delight of learning the skills and techniques of welding. She was playing with fire, practically and figuratively, as we shall see later… and she loved it! What she loved also was to play games consisting in exhibiting herself in public places with my complicity and for our mutual sexual excitement. All started in Atlanta where we were going to spend week-ends from bars to night clubs and strip joints. There, as perfect strangers, she liked to dress very light and provocative, usually without underwear. At bars she used to pose on high stools in a way to invite and entice the male and female population around…for a conversation! In night clubs, dancing was the means to reveal her body in swing moves which almost ripped her dress off her gorgeous body. I was never farther than about twenty feet away, for her protection… just in case, and enjoying erections as never before. Once, at "Cheetah 3", the most popular strip joint of Atlanta, she wished to participate in a table dance with another female striper in the darkness of our reserved seating in the dining area of the club… but was strongly dissuaded to do so by a security guard with no sense of humor! In Greenville, we did a little bit of it also, in similar places, although it was more risky, since encountering unwelcome "gossipy" people was very possible… but it never happened! The most enjoyable one was at the mall. There, dressed with a school-girl mini dress and a thong, she was bending over from time to time, as if checking something at the bottom of shop windows, and by doing so, flashing her butts to the public. What a sexual treat it was! Upon return at home, we rushed in to make love even before the door has closed behind us… When, earlier in the game, I questioned her about her appetite for exhibitionism, she answered that once, when her father made her walk around the block, naked, to shame her, she felt an orgasm - not knowing at that time what it was - and, since then, was eager to reproduce it… Exhibitionism was her adult way to re-enact the naked walk in the street and the subsequent orgasm build-up!

When things finally started to slow down, after several months of joyful excitement, we began to look at joining a naturist club in the area. There was nothing close by. The nearest clubs were either in Georgia, one in north of Atlanta and, for the other, east of

Augusta in: "Graniteville", in South Carolina. We visited both places and elected to membership in Graniteville at: "Uncle Henry's". There we met Pam and George, a couple from Atlanta with whom we paid several visits to: "Hidden Valley" in North Atlanta, but our preference was Uncle Henry's for its friendly atmosphere and attractive landscape. We were driving there as often as business permitted. After a short while, we knew everybody, including visitors from Greenville who were almost neighbors. One day, I received an intriguing phone call from an individual named: "Jack". Jack lived in Cleveland S.C. in a mountain-lake cabin at the foothills of the "Blue Ridge" in the Appalachian Mountains, off of Highway 11, the scenic route of upstate S.C., forty minutes from Greenville. He introduced himself as the owner of a 100 acres country side property with a man-made lake of 20 acres. He then followed this comment by divulging that he was a naturist himself and that he got my name from Uncle Henry's, whom he was an acquaintance and occasional former visitor, while he was busy building his new place in Cleveland. At that time, his wife did not want to hear anything about naturism although Jack's dream was to convert her, one day, to his lifestyle. That day never happened. A couple of years in his trade, as a builder, Jack's wife died from a cancer and he found himself single and almost alone in his "green paradise" if it was not for his son Chet and wife who lived next to his place on the same property. He offered that Chantal and I come to visit him and get acquainted to each other. We accepted with great joy and, for few minutes, wondered why the Divine Providence was so generous with us!

On that hot Sunday of August, we finally arrived at Jack's cabin after wondering, many times, if we were not lost in spite of following his directions to the letter. The place was very secluded, hard to find and difficult to access due to the bad condition of the dirt road, but at the last turn in the woods, facing the lake, the view was gorgeous, almost unreal… indeed a paradise on earth! We have seen beautiful places before but that one was truly unique, nested in between two ranges of rolling hills ending at the lake at the bottom of the valley. The view was breathtaking. For a moment we stood by the car staring at the place, not even paying attention to Jack, who, from his front porch, was hailing us a warm welcome. The first contact with Jack was comparable to "love at first sight". The man was friendly, easy going and outgoing. He talked about his defunct wife, his love for her and promised to take us to the place she was buried in at: "Traveler's rest", a small town some ten miles away from his cabin. He explained that they lived in Florida, where they were both born and grew up, until his wife got a lung cancer which, the doctors said, it would help cure if they moved to a place in the mountains. And so they did, in their early fifties. The difference in age between him and us was about twenty years. He could have been our father although he did not look his age. The bond we established that day never died and even today is still alive in our minds some fifteen years after his death at seventy five… and us nearing seventy… but I am digressing. As mentioned earlier, Jack's dream was to create a nudist club in his vast property. His managerial skills, as a builder, should have helped him to achieve that goal but, in short, it never happened! After several attempts to officially "OPEN", a noticeable lack of discipline, personal and financial, always led to the demise of the club. Finally, sick and broke, Jack put the property for sale. When he asked me if I would be interested to buy it I could hardly hide the pain I felt saying: NO. I had the credit and the money to buy it, on the spot, but our immigration status and professional situation were not allowing us to make this kind of decision. My green card was not issued yet, although applied for, and ultimately, I was at the mercy of the Company to either stay in the US or face another transfer on a no time notice! I was frustrated! Things turned out for the better when an acquaintance of Jack by the name of Gilbert (Gil in short) purchased the whole property... Gil and his wife Sarah, who lived in Cleveland, were both teachers; him in the primary school of Travelers' rest and her in Greenville at: "Stone Academy". Both were from Florida and met Jack when they moved to Cleveland S.C. which they preferred to Florida... weather-wise! We met them a couple of times at Jack's place and were once invited to their cottage in Cleveland for the first birthday of their daughter: "Amy". At the time they bought the property, they allowed Jack to stay in his cabin until he dies and, for us, to continue to lease from them the land onto which we build our own cabin in 1989. We built the cabin with Jack's approval and support to promote what could have been a model cabin for potential nudist settlers. Size wise it could accommodate a couple with two kids. The unit had electricity, inner plumbing with running water and a septic tank for sewage. Some nudists were interested but nothing ever materialized due to a lack of seriousness on Jack's part to follow through. Actually we were the first and last nudist settlers and are still enjoying, today, "the Little Cabin", as we call it. As far as Gil and Sarah, their plan was to build a cabin, sensibly bigger than their cottage in Cleveland, on the opposite side of the lake from Jack's. In the meantime, in order to save money, they decide to move to the "Blue Cabin" (because it was painted in blue), which, for a while, was Jack's son "Chet's" dwelling, when they both moved together from Florida. The Blue Cabin became vacant when Chet and his wife, claiming to be: "Southern Baptist Fundamentalists", deserted the place in disagreement with Jack's decision to turn the property into a nudist camp. At this point in time we were three families on the property: Jack in his own cabin, Gil, Sarah and Amy in the

Blue Cabin and us in the Little Cabin. We were spending weekends there as often as possible. Due to the recent history of the place, nudity was optional although we tried not to practice it when Gil and Sarah were on the premises. They did give it a try once at one of the several "openings" of Jack's nudist club but did not seem to have enjoyed it too much and consequently never showed up again during nudist events. While we were respecting our new landlords' tacit preference, on their land, we continued to practice our lifestyle elsewhere, mainly during our vacation time. Places we have visited were: "Cypress Cove" in Kissimmee near Orlando, "Sunshine Gardens" in Jupiter, "Paradise Lakes" and "Lake Como" in Land O'Lake, north of Tampa, all in Florida; "Indian Hills" in Slidell, Louisiana, not to mention the already mentioned "Uncle Henry's", in Graniteville SC and "Hidden Valley", north of Atlanta, in Georgia. Also, worth of mentioning, are two barefoot cruises of seven days each on a sail boat manned by "Captain Fred" and his mate "Sandy". From Clearwater to Tarpon Springs, to Sarasota and the isle of Anticot, days were spent navigating leisurely in the nude, sunbathing, fishing and scuba diving. The first cruise was with Chantal and Michael and the second one without Michael but with Pam from Atlanta and her new boyfriend: "Hubert", a French Canadian chiropractor.

CHAPTER 12

WHEN MELANCHOLY MEETS NOSTALGIA

At this point in time we were well established in Greenville. We had obtained our "green card" and were at the threshold of becoming American citizens. The latter would definitively stabilize our standing in America. Although sponsored by Michelin, the path to permanent residency was long and stressful due to a lack of precise schedule and personal communication with the INS. We were at the receiving end with no control over the timeline and final outcome. Actually an administrative glitch on the part of our sponsor caused a delay in granting our permanent residency on time and forced Michelin to grant me an "investor visa" in order to keep myself and my family in the USA prior to obtaining the green card. Needless to say that this situation created undue tensions between Chantal and I who was blaming me for not being in control (as if it was my fault) or too weak to fight the Company's negligence. All of that was irritating and tiring and created a climate of tension and distrust between us which, for a while, gravely damaged our, otherwise, lovely relationship. Feeling alone and with no support from her, I began to let myself surrender to melancholy. Nostalgia, as a consequence of it, started to haunt me to the point, at times, of regretting having left France, for such a poor outcome! Michael, after graduating from Greenville High School with four years of Navy Junior ROTC under his belt, was in his second year at Spartanburg Methodist College (SMC) and well in his way to graduate in Psychology before transferring to a four year university. Chantal was pretty happy with her welded master pieces, which were encumbering our house and garage, while waiting for being exhibited for sale in private art galleries, but mainly with her new modeling job. Being in the spotlight was always her dream life. Although humble, she was proud of her looks and almost "orgasmic" when she was doing layouts showing more skin than clothing for local shops competing with "Victoria secrets"! Clyde, the welding instructor, talked her into doing modeling. He was her coach and the one who opened for her the doors of modeling agencies and professional photographic studios. For her, showing off in glamour magazines and big stores catalogs and advertisement brochures, in the great nation of America, was a kind of achievement which was close to the glorification she was often dreaming of but thought she was unworthy of… In addition to her metal crafts and modeling shots, she took courses at the Greenville Tech to become a French language substitute teacher. That became her main activity and, very rapidly, her life was full to the point of neglecting her domestic tasks as a housewife. As for me, life became routine… not to say boring! All the activities of my new job were under tight control. I earned the respect and recognition for a job well done. My long hours of the beginning became shorter and I was looking for some extra professional activities to fill the hours of emptiness when I was returning to an empty home, especially when Michael hit the road to college and decided to reside on the campus.

Back in 1987, I noticed that my weight of 165 lbs, ten years earlier, began to flirt with the 190 mark. I was offended by the realization that my "six pack" like muscled belly was turning into a "beer keg" like fat one. I decided to go to the gym to contain the damages! I member-shipped at: "Gold Gym" and, by doing so, promised to myself to regain my earlier sporty looks. This new program of one hour at a time, three times a week, really changed my life and I was looking forward to getting there, religiously, for the sake of health but also for the ten minutes of relaxation in the burning sauna followed by another ten minutes in the boiling Jacuzzi… and then the soothing under a cold shower. Though, that was not enough. Reminiscing of my years as a parachutist in the military and a onetime recreational dual flight on a glider from the mighty mountain of: "Puy de Dome" in Auvergne, France, I decided to join the local gliding club of: "Glassy Mountain" with Jim and john as my instructors. The guys were great; however, the scary mountains of the Appalachian Blue Ridge and the capricious winds of the Carolinas never gave me the thrill I have experienced in France. To the contrary, each flight built up more anguish and fear that the next one might be fatal as it was to one guy who died from his injuries and another who remained paralyzed… I quit gliding and, to compensate, decided to return to my primal love of the water sports that I discovered in the river Allier and which included fishing, tubing, swimming, snorkeling, free diving and now: scuba diving! I joined a local scuba shop and began my twenty hours/four weeks training, twice a week, in a nine feet deep swimming pool and final graduation in lake: "Jockassee", a mountain man-made lake, in the Blue Ridge of South Carolina bordering North Carolina. After several lake dives in the border artificial lakes between South Carolina and Georgia, my first ocean dive was during the long weekend of Labor Day of 1988. "Will", the dive master and "Connie", his wife, took eight of us in their van and drove, quasi non-stop for twelve hours, to the town of North Palm Beach, Florida, where we met another dive shop which took us to the sea off of Phil Foster Park, adjacent to Singer Island which houses the high end dwellings of Riviera Beach and Palm Beach Shores. After few hours of sleep and a good brunch, we went diving in the afternoon off the coast of Palm Beach with the towers of the historic hotel named: "The Breakers", still visible in the distant background. During this first encounter with the area just described, I did not know that it will become, some twenty seven years later, the landing place and playground of my retirement years…

Living in Greenville was not the best place for scuba diving. Even Charleston and Myrtle Beach, on the coast, were not known as world class scuba diving spots! Apart from the lakes, where scuba divers were congregating for the sole pleasure to go deep under, mostly to discover barren bottoms, or test their equipment before a trip to the sea, the nearest best place was Florida. As for me, I was privileged to live on a lake which, on occasion, gave me the opportunity to go under to test my skills and equipment in about twenty feet of water, right at the bottom of the dam's mid length, where the overflow vane was located, without having to schedule a trip to the lakes with a diving shop.

In spite of all of these activities, I did not feel happy and fulfilled as I was in France. Even the joy and fascination of the discovery of the "American life" during the earlier years in the USA were gone. We had a lot of acquaintances but no real friends. Our lifestyle also changed visibly. Chantal began to show some embarrassment when being criticized, by some of her "good" Southern Carolinian female friends, for being a nudist, a four times men's magazine nude model and an occasional swinger, things that she confessed as being natural for her and with no shame at all. Although, at first, she was excused for her "French" bold statement of her lifestyle (which might have raised some jealousy as well), overtime, the "good" friends did convince her that she was living a devilish life and succeeded in having her to promise to enroll in a Baptist bible study. After a while and mainly because she was looking for company, she submitted to their demand to join their church and attend Bible studies on a regular basis. As she said to me, at one time, now I know what: "being born again" means!

Speaking of "being born again", I recall that the concept also overwhelmed me on November 2nd 1995, precisely, when the explosive cocktail of "material libertine life" and "spiritual godly life" burst into my face without notice. In the Catholic tradition and contrary to common assumption, November 1st is not the celebration of the "Dead", but that of "All Saints". Celebrated on the 2nd of November is the day of the dead. Well, that day, I died spiritually, to resurrect to a new reality which I will try to describe and explain to the best I can...

If I "saw the light" or "was born again" on that day, the process by which it has started began one week earlier. We were in the cabin by the lake where I was fishing with no success. At one point I decided to borrow a book from my friend Jack since I forgot to bring any literature from home for the week-end. Although it was not in my habit not to carry enough reading materials to alternate with my hours of meditation while fishing, this time, it was the case! At Jack's place, I immediately spotted a book seating on his coffee table. Jack offered that I take it, although he was himself on it. He said that he will catch up later when I return the book the following week-end. Upon returning to the cabin, I settled comfortably on the couch and, unconsciously, began what became a process of initiation and inspiration of unimaginable consequences…

It was about 12:00 noon when Chantal returned from a long walk in the mountains, to stay in shape, but also, I suspect, to clear her head from what happened the night before. The night before we were bickering, as usual, about, according to her, my pathetic independence that always prevented us from doing things together as, according to her, all the other couples did! In fact, in the USA, she became more and more independent from me concerning her personal and social life but more dependent on me than ever concerning her domestic life, which, by the way, she had entirely abdicated to me. The disconnect between her needs and mine could be summarized as follow: hers were the headaches of coordinating the meetings at the church, the invitations to our house of perfect nice strangers for diner and conversation, the cocktail parties at the museum where all the "snobbish" of Greenville were gathering, the monthly attendance to the "Peace Center" for the performing arts; mine were the worries of getting a second mortgage for the house, loans for the cars and Michael's scholarship, more loans to restore the old house, not enough time to follow-up on Michael's studies and to keep up with the basic requirements of home accounting and… paying the bills! Obviously my reluctance to fit her schedule and her contempt for my petty concerns were irreconcilable. In this foul context, in the eyes of our entourage, she became the brainy adorable socialite and I the typical rude redneck…

For me, in order to avoid being talked into participating in her "social headaches" was to create a "vacuum" around me in order to preserve some semblance of independence. I needed some free space. I was chocking for a breath of air! My technique to create such a vacuum was to either give her: "the silent treatment" or mocking loudly what she was saying until she shut up. I was very uncomfortable with my irate irrational behavior but could not accept, every time she was picking a fight, that I should be always wrong and she, always right! In spite of all the excuses I was using to justify her attitude towards me, I was convinced that she was picking on me just for the pleasure of enraging me and consequently using my derived unkindness towards her as a pretext to "spit" on me, time and time again, all the resentment she has stored, from her birth, in her disturbed heart. Actually I felt as being the scapegoat for all of her past, present and (why not!) even future miseries. Among the excuses I was fabricating in order to salvage my love for her was the fact that she was physically and verbally abused during her upbringing in a dysfunctional family. Another one was that her education in a mixed culture and during the revolutionary war of independence of Algeria was limited. In fact she was ashamed of her poor colloquial French spoken in Algeria (referred to as: "pataouet" by the French from France) which she fought to improve from the moment she landed in France. I also suspected that, in the beginning of our stay in the US, her broken English did not help to establish her as a National in spite of her claiming to be more American than French… In the face of the struggle she was confronting, she has used her charm to overcome some of it, in society, while attempting to diminish me, privately, in order to be up to par… needless to say that I suspected also her Baptist bunch to have absolved her for her sexual sins by charging me for her bewilderments. In the middle of the fights, my typical answer was, as already mentioned: indifference, intimidation and humiliation. After the "storms", which became chronic, she was in my arms, proclaiming her love for me, her need for intimacy and above all her desire to see me change for the better if I would only listen to her. Literally, she was begging me to admit that something was wrong with me and to recognize, with no doubt, that she was on the right track and that I was not! I had a hard time to surrender to her repeated requests to change but, ultimately, I always let go for the sake of the good time we have had together in the past… The alternative was to leave her, knowing that she will never meet me half way, and I did not want that to happen for the sake of our son Michael. Also because, even all lives have their moments of pain, angst, trouble and strife (mine being no exception), on balance, the "rewards" have far, far out weighted the "punishments". Despite the occasional resentments, the most consistent fact remained the long relationship I have had with my gorgeous, loved and loving wife!

No matter how painful it was, I promised that I will do my best to satisfy her demands. In all of these nasty fights, where I saw myself whining and never winning, made me, at times, feel like an idiot. I, the first of the class, the leader, the rational guy, was at a loss in front of her arguments loaded with her version of Southern Baptist definition of love… which I hated! My behavior, according to her and her counselors at the bible studies, was the reflection of a mean evil spirit loaded with perverse and vicious intentions. In spite of all my intellectual efforts to comprehend her motives I could not shoehorn myself in her mysterious soul. In short, she was the victim, a status and a birthmark, and I was the molester!

From the day of the last fight to the 2nd of November, I was restless, trying to understand why these things were happening, why so often and self entertaining, even without provocation, as if they had a life of their own. I knew the questions but ignored the answers. The reading of Jack's book began to shed some light on possible answers. I started fast reading as a hungry man feeds his mouth with both hands. It was like somebody knew my story and was answering my needs for understanding. Finally I had my answers…

The title of the book was: "Meditation on the divine legitimacy of man", with a subtitle: "by the bet of divinity and the reflex of kindness for the salvational revolution". If the reading did not remove all of the lingering negative nostalgia of the recent past, it did undoubtedly, kill the anxiety which was hurting me to the point of living in constant fear of another fight.

CHAPTER 13

THE NEW: "NORMAL"

Life was going on punctuated with mainly work and vacations dedicated to travel. In addition to our annual trips to France to visit family and friends, other trips, during the year, were targeted to discover the world of the Americas and its history. The laundry list of our adventures included Belize and Guatemala in central America; Mexico, Cozumel and its Yucatan peninsula; "the Maritimes" made up of Nova Scotia, New Brunswick, Prince Edward Island and Cape Breton, the province of Quebec, in Canada; Hawaii and Honolulu by the Waikiki beach; the Caribbean Islands of Puerto Rico, St. Martin, Martinique, Guadeloupe, Barbados, Jamaica and the Cayman Islands and, Cherry on the cake: Peru. Peru with the unforgettable Cusco, The market of Pissac, the sacred site of Sexawaman, the Inca's capital of Machu-Pichu, the Nazca lines, the Pisco-Paracas candelabra on the mountain-dunes of Huakashina near Ica and the Galapagos like islands not to mention Lima. Lima and its Spanish architecture and favellas and Iquitos in the Amazon Jungle by the mighty river of the same name where still live some of the primitive Indians in South America. Also, sneaking out of our French visits, we went to Germany, Checko-Slovakia, Poland and Lithuania…

In the meantime, after High School graduation, Michael went to SMC to become a social worker upon graduating in psychology, as he said: to help abused children… He did not quite finish his second year when psychology caught up with him. In a burst of violent anger he was hospitalized at Spartanburg Regional Hospital, for a month, and was diagnosed with bipolar disorder…

In the meantime, Chantal became a devoted Southern Baptist and a full time professional substitute French Teacher spending most of her time with her church and school friends and Clyde, her welding instructor and modeling coach.

In the meantime, I changed jobs several times, became a full time American employee as opposed to being a French expatriate. I lost my status as, what some Americans jealously called: a "French protégé", and had to prove myself, as a project manager and lead engineer, in every new projects I was assigned to… specially, since Michelin purchased the bankrupt US companies of Uniroyal, BF Goodrich and their associated brands. For the last decade of my career, before retiring, my job consisted in: "Michelinizing" the new acquisitions or contribute to their elimination from the "Michelin Family". Yes, life was going on with a lot of time and energy spent in salvaging what was left of Michael's sanity, in deflecting a lot of blame and finger pointing because of Michael's condition and also in the abuse of too much booze and smoking for me and booze, smoking and diet pills for her! For Chantal, she ended up spending a couple of months in different detoxification centers. For me, I quit smoking, cold turkey, which almost killed instantly my propensity to drinking after work and much less on week-ends. Michael went to "Gateway House of Greenville" where he started a lengthy process of recovery. Gateway House is a rehabilitation center for mentally ill individuals by means of work and internal social interactions. As a qualified member and a beneficiary of "Medicaid" and SSI (social security income) he was also provided a subsidized low rent apartment so that he could live a totally independent life within the framework of the institution. Suddenly we became empty nesters although Michael was living on the same street at about a quarter mile from our house.

The new normal consisted in having Michael and being with him as often as possible while trying to reconnect with Chantal upon my returns from business trips which were consuming almost 30% of my life away from home. I loved my new independence and the sense of freedom at work fully justified as a successful business supporter of the Company. Besides, and to a certain extend to excuse my absence from home, I became the prodigal breadwinner showering his family with presents, going out to restaurants and places of entertainment more often than ever! Business took me to Romania, Italy, Columbia (South America), Thailand, the: U. K. (United Kingdom), Ireland, Germany, Mexico, most of Canada, adding to the Maritimes and Quebec the province of Ontario and lately: Poland. These trips expanded my vision of the world in a way I have never believed was possible! Actually, at that time, for me, home, my couple and family became secondary to my new obsessive addiction to travel, international and domestic alike and the excitement of meeting people of different cultures, races and languages. Traveling was my ego's trip! I learned Spanish and perfected my native Polish which is spoken or understood to different degrees in the entire Slavic Central and Eastern parts of Europe.

The world became my new home and my business acquaintances, my new family.

Strangely, because of the feud we have entertained for years, the limited moments of togetherness with my wife created a new situation void of bickering, complaints or nagging… What a change compared to what was our relationship in a more sedentary condition! Actually, slowly but surely our re-unions became more like dating again. A true rekindling of the flame of love took full effect after a couple of years of my globe-trotter's escapades which, for her, was the perfect opportunity to go further along with her social life… without me and without having to excuse me!

The cabin by the lake was the focus of our new torrid sexual love-life and the romantic love nest of our renewed attraction to each other. Jack's book on "Meditation" (which I purchased to have it available at all times for reference) was also present and in full view on our cabin's coffee table. The book was like a fetish, the anchor and the guide of our new "born again lives" in a world where, it seemed, we were dropped by chance, in a universe indifferent to us, without a road map to show us where to go or a user's manual indicating how to manage life and our environment… According to the book, it seemed that our choice was limited to either look for the virtues of the "Kingdom" of God or the vices of the "Darkness" of Evil. In our state of mind then, it is needless to say that we chose what the book was pointing to as: "the Kingdom"!

The book was so true to God, life, love and sex that all of our thoughts, words and actions were impregnated by the essence of its teachings. We read it together and spent hours making sense of it all as well as questioning ourselves on the direction we have decided to take. Although some passages were too obscure to be comprehended at that time, it became evident, as an example, intuitively not rationally, that there is life after death. The support for this intuition was based on the fact that there is life after death, for a fetus, which has spent nine months of his first life in the "liquid environment" of his mother's womb and died to that "liquid" life before being forcefully projected in the "gaseous" world of planet earth. Similarly, we deducted that we will be living again in the "ethereal atmosphere of Heaven" after our earthly death…

My belief in death as "the gateway to heaven" is explained by the death of Jesus. Beginning in "Genesis" which claims that, because of his fault, Adam was condemned to death and that his condemnation was passed on to me through no fault of my own… Jesus, in His benevolence and His pity for humanity, decided to save my life by dying in my stead so that I could regain Adam's lost "paradisiacal life", forever, and therefore live a "happy life", down here and now on earth, with Him resurrected, in me, and later, out there, in heaven, through Him… if I only believe in Him and follow his commandments.

For me, it became evident that Jesus is living in me and that we are living together as one. Consequently, every time I am dissatisfied with some adverse circumstances, I am asking Him, as the book instructed me: to always remind me that no frustration or exaltation will ever happen to me that He and I cannot handle together! I knew that He was working through me and was praying that His Will be my will, not mine alone, now and always. Last but not least, I was asking Him to remember that I was working for Him and pleaded that He would work through me, for His glory; for His glory is my success in my journey from me to Him, one day at a time, every day, beginning with each new day.

The experience of God as the glue keeping our marriage from falling apart and the aphrodisiac for the near death orgasms of our renewed love-making was so real that His presence was palpable, if not visible, in each of us and in the environment around us. The cabin was the temple were our love lived and thrived to the point of becoming one love and one life in two persons. At times, I was wondering if the life in the Garden of Eden, in Genesis, was not a mirror image of our place by the mountain lake! Actually, life was like a rebirth to love every day while awaiting the birth of God in us, which would definitely, conform us to His image… one day!

With simple faith, we knew that God was living in us, on earth, and that we will live, eternally, through him, in heaven. With simple faith, we were convinced that we do not need God and Christ if we believe there is no life after death but that we definitively need Him, otherwise, since He is the only one, on earth, who organized his death and resurrection in order to prove that there is an afterlife. We were convinced that Jesus was the earthly: "Avatar of God" who reconciled man with Himself, by Himself, as the "chosen son of God" as opposed to the Jewish belief that their Messiah (yet to come) would reconcile man with God by enforcing the application of the laws of Moses by His "chosen people". With simple faith we knew that no one is supposed to understand the law but that it suffices to obey it. That obedience is simple faith. That simple faith is to believe without seeing; to be convinced while seeking understanding; to know without being able to prove and to surrender to God with serenity. To us, the "New" Testament was our only bible. The "Old" Testament was merely a book of Jewish history and of discovery of: psychology, sociology and morality, supposedly inspired by God for the survival and the betterment of the Jewish people, or, more generally, an ensemble of ancient human scriptures which makes God say authoritatively what man wants to hear in order to justify his behavior! Respect for the Old Testament, by us, was only dictated by Jesus' statement that He came: "not to abolish, but to accomplish"…

The biggest accomplishment of our rediscovery of Christ through the book of: "Meditation", was to count our blessings. Remembering how we worked our way through the INS was not a small feat since it took us ten years to become American citizens! The hurdles, frustration and the unimaginable patience required to follow through was squarely attributed to God without whom nothing would have been possible. At times we were ready to quit the process and leave the United States, not to return to France, but more romantically to one of the French islands of the Caribbean archipelago. Another blessing of "Biblical" proportion was when Michael ran away from Gateway House and ended up homeless in the cold winter of 2007 in Saint Louis, Missouri. For three weeks we were with no news of him, although I reported him to the FBI as a missing mentally handicapped and vulnerable person. When, one evening, the telephone rang and a voice asked if I would take a collect call, instinctively I knew that Michael was at the other end of the line. We greeted each other and Michael begged that I come to pick him up the next day. Early, the following morning, Chantal and I were heading to Jefferson City where he gave us an address to meet him at. He was there and the sight of him moved me to tears. I knew that all the time spent driving safely in winter conditions and finally finding the place he was at, at night, without GPS, was the work of our caring God. Also, our reconciliation, as a couple, was so real and sincere that Chantal volunteered to confess having had a couple of flings and several short lived one night stand affairs along with the more permanent one with Clyde… shortly after he died. I did not go to the funerals since I was on a business trip that day, but accepted, upon my return, to accompany her to his grave for a moment of silent reflection. He was twenty years older than her and their relationship lasted for at least a decade. There was no rancor or jealousy. I was at peace with myself and that was all that counted. I knew that here also, my God, who promised me His peace, was present during this "uneasy" time. Uneasy it was because, in spite of our wild love life of the distant past, that kind of relationship was not in our "culture". It was not swinging with its openness and complicity but also with its rules and limitations. It was not: "sex, drug and rock and roll", as practiced by the "Hippy Baby Boomers", which consisted mainly of binge drinking leading to semi-conscious orgy fornication. It was not even the summer flirting in Ile du Levant which led us, knowingly and for a while, to the slippery slope of short term consensual cheating. Instead it was secret, hidden, unspoken. Quickies or long term… It looked like a vicious pursuit of egotistic self gratification, by self serving pleasure at the expense of multiple interchangeable estranged partners. In my eyes, for a woman, it was nymphomania, at best, or "selective nonprofit prostitution", at worst, but, after all, not so much different from men's pursuit of adulterous relations due to compulsive sexual obsession. Actually, she took advantage of my absence from home and, in her case, it surely was something to expect with regard to her appetite for sex and the freedom we enjoyed in our past open sex life. As for me, it was just another confirmation of my teenage understanding of women's sexuality which is that women will use, abuse and misuse the advantage of their innate "God given sex appeal", not only to satisfy their legitimate instinct of procreation (for a limited time) but also to fulfill their sexual fantasies (at all times) at the expense of their cupid (or stupid) "lovers"! An unkind observer would probably call them: "born sluts"…

Anyway, this moment of disappointment passed away and things returned to normal after a couple of week-ends of sexual abstinence and the insistent reiterated requests from her for total forgiveness, which I kept granting sincerely!

The biggest blessing of all happened when Michael, after resettling his life with Gateway House, became a motivational speaker and fundraiser for the organization but also for: "United Way". He was chosen by the administration of Gateway House to present the mission of the institution to businesses in the area and to encourage others, like him, but living in "half way" dwellings, to get "off their ass" and join in active participation in the many activities of the House. He was so good and so dedicated that very soon he became an auditor and began to travel across the USA and Europe (Stockholm in Sweden and Paris in France) to audit and accredit other "Houses" modeled after Gateway House of Greenville. In addition to his job description he was also invited to attend meetings and seminars, as a faculty member, for his continuous betterment as a speaker, a trainer and a "customer service" associate providing guidance and support to other "houses' members" by means of direct contact, phone and the Internet. His unpaid job was more rewarding than any paid job he could have dreamed of, had he graduated from college. It is with great pride that I have placarded a section of a wall in my study with framed pictures of him with VIPs such as the governor of South Carolina, the CEO of Michelin North America and others, less famous, like state senators, representatives and almost all members of United Way's and Gateway House's boards of directors. Michael's life, which once, was gloom and doom, was now in full bloom! I always heard that if one can help himself that God would help him too, but through Michael, I realized that God also provides abundantly to those who cannot!

Last but not least of all the blessings was my return to Sunday Mass. For years, although Chantal continued to hang with her Southern Baptist friends in Bible studies, she seldom missed Mass on Sundays at Saint Mary's Catholic Church on Washington Street. Surely by tradition, although I cannot judge her deeper motives, if any! She begged me to go, if for no better reason than to show the good example to our son who was going to catechism in preparation for "confirmation". Since, for about fifteen years, I kept refusing to go, claiming that I lost faith in the God of Christians I stood my ground by asserting that I was on a search of true spirituality and that I would eventually return to Christianity, or definitely stay away from it, when my search has exhausted all the reasonable human attempts to find the truth.

Finding the truth was my new hobby and pastime. Through readings, TV programs, movies and internet zapping, I surfed on most of all known religions, from Primitives to Ancient World Mythologies and organized political Cults. The Asian approach, to me, was the least attractive because of the basic concept of multiple reincarnations (including in animals) which did not sit well with me. Besides, "Kama sutra" was very attractive as part of their culture. Buddhism, though, grabbed my imagination. Just for a little while, mind you, because of its intuitive understanding of the notion of "relativity". Notion that later was scientifically demonstrated by Albert Einstein. It opened a window on the "invisible". However, the lack of "Supernatural" endeavors turned me away from a man (Buddha) who, after all, was just that: a man and nothing more. I finally stored him in my Pantheon of idols which I greatly respected as men and martyrs like: "Vercingetorix" who once, in the name of freedom, vanquished the Roman Emperor Cesar in the battle of the Gaul (which later became France) in 52 BC; "Clovis", the first king of France who got baptized by Saint Remi and made France a Christian nation; "Charlemagne", the last French Emperor of the Western Roman Empire, who made school free and mandatory for the enlightenment of his people; "Johan of Arc" who, in the name of God, fought the English off of France at the end of the 100 years war between France and England; "Napoleon Bonaparte", the emperor who saved the French Revolution of 1989 and the declaration of human rights and put France first by conquering Europe; "Gandhi" (the India's Hindu) who applied without restrain the concept of non-violence and consequently liberated India from the British; "General De Gaulle", who restored the dignity of France by joining the allies against the Nazis and their French "collaborators", during WWII; "Martin Luther King" and "John Kennedy" (the Americans), who gave up their lives for the promotion of black human rights; "Solyenitsin" (the Russian), "Lech Walesa", and "Pope John Paul II" (the Polish), who contributed to the fall of the communism... to name a few.

Islam revealed itself as a scam by claiming to be a religion for the sole purpose of imperialism by means of military conquest (the Jihad), stealing from the Jews' and Christians' scriptures. Its strategy was, first, to convert Jews and Christians to Islam and then use them, as converted Muslims, to conquer the world, in the name of "Allah", by the sword! "Mohamed" knew where to find converts in Jews tired of waiting for a "Messiah" who was slow to come and disgusted Christians repulsed by the immorality of the Papacy. Mohamed was a shroud politician but he was just that: a politician and nothing more. As for the "Koran", as an "inspired by God" governmental constitution, I found much better ones in the lay political environment and therefore discarded it. Yet, as part of the Arab culture I enjoyed reading the heavy erotically loaded stories of "The Thousand and One Nights" and liked the propensity of Arabs to be polygamists. But that was not enough to keep me interested in Islam in spite of the seventy two virgins promised, at death, to the righteous ones...

To my surprise I delighted in Primitive religions and Ancient Mythologies. The latter for the imagination displayed in associating the "Supernatural" to the "Natural" where men were gods and gods were men... What a great revelation! From it I drew the conviction that: "God" is, by definition, the fundamental principle of "life" as well as the "metamorphosis" of life in "bodies" either of supernatural beings as angels or of natural ones as humans on earth and saints in heaven. For the former, the spirits of the primitives, although mainly in the form of animals, were very similar to the protective angels and the revered saints of our contemporary culture, and very popular in the Catholic tradition, and therefore I saw and admired them as the forerunners of many more elaborate religions.

The least intellectual religions were those who fascinated me the most. And speaking of simple teachings, what about the "parables": Christ's teachings? Nothing can be more powerful than a parable, a tale for kids with the power to teach adults! I re-read the gospels and fell again in love with the "greatest story ever told", a story about the birth, life, deeds, death and resurrection of Jesus Christ. The very one I thought I had lost faith in, was coming back at me after many years away from Him, as the real thing which explains and justifies everything. Suddenly, mass, seen as a boring routine which keeps repeating itself, made the greatest sense of all. It revealed itself to me as the recurring public celebration of the live presence of Christ resurrected in the Eucharist, down here on earth, until His second coming in the resurrected "Body of Saints", beyond there in Haven. Christ's second coming was clearly His future metamorphosis in the body of saints as it is, in His present one, in the soul of the human "called ones".

This in-depth realization convinced me that, even if the Christ I believed in did not exist, this is Him, who I believe in, who does exist and of whom I will draw the strength and wisdom to love till the end! As the French philosopher "Voltaire" said: "if God did not exist, one should have invented Him"...

Another realization which hit me like a ton of bricks was that the "Communion on the bread and wine", as the body and blood of Christ, was in fact the "good meal" of my youth's understanding, as being the gift of "enjoyment", that God wanted us to have to celebrate the life of Jesus in order to enjoy our own life down here, on earth, and later in Heaven.

From these realizations, I concluded that the Catholic liturgy was the most appropriate to make the most of Christ, on earth, and for that, I never missed a Sunday mass… or say: never intentionally.

CHAPTER 14

RETIRING FROM ACTIVE DUTY

Before I knew it, retirement was knocking at the door. In spite of my love of traveling and passion for directing projects, big and small, international and domestic, I began to think about leaving this agitated life for another one more calm and away from the heat of the action. Working with the bureaucratic administrations of Michelin-France and Michelin in the USA, which ultimately would deliver the pensions I financially contributed to and therefore was entitled to, was a challenge worthy of my most challenging projects! I had to deal with the French Government for the years I have worked under a French Michelin contract in France and then in the USA, as an expatriate, in my earlier years with the Company and also to manage the coverage by Michelin-America and the American Social Security Administration for the remaining working years of my carrier as an American employee. Needless to say that there was no common ground in the process of obtaining the retirement money from each country and therefore, working on both pensions at the same time, was like passing, back and forth, from one world to another, one culture to another, one social ideology to another… After about a year of effort and patience, all was lined up for the grabs! Since we decided to retire in the USA, back in 2002, we sold our house in France and invested the proceeds in a townhouse at "Abacoa", a brand new subdivision of Jupiter in Florida, which was in the design stages at the time of purchase. When the house was finished and up for rent in early 2005, it was unfortunate that we could not rent it because of the ongoing construction of adjacent blocks with all the nuisances it carried along. After three months of trial, we gave up and sold it for a net profit that has exceeded my current yearly salary after tax at that time! Immediately we re-invested part of that money in a more modest townhouse, in the subdivision of "Jupiter village" next door to Abacoa. The house was rented within a week of posting for the great amount of $850 per month considering that it was composed of only one bedroom and one full bath. At retirement time, the ultimate plans were to sale the houses in Greenville and Jupiter and reinvest the proceeds in a house, "on the water", somewhere in Palm Beach County. In 2010 when I decided to retire on May 22, forty two years and four days from the signing of my contract with Michelin, the housing market was at its lowest point following the financial crash of 2008/2009. Selling at that time was not an option; therefore the alternative solution was either to stay in Greenville until the housing market recovered or use the house in Jupiter to begin enjoying the warm weather of South Florida. After notifying my last tenant to leave the premises, one month prior to our move to Florida, we opted for a compromise which consisted of traveling back and forth every three months between the two places. This arrangement helped to transition from our thirty years residence in Greenville to a new place fairly alien to us in spite of our frequent visits as vacationers. As vacationers we saw Florida through the rosy glamour glasses of tourists. As part time residents we changed them for the less fascinating ones of owners with all the responsibilities ranging from questioning and paying utility bills to dealing with the HOA (Home Owners Association) for house improvement approvals, with the city's building department for construction permits… not to mention negotiations with the IRS for property tax exemption or assurances (because of the hurricanes) to find the best coverage at the lowest price. There were times when we did not go to the beach, at least once a week, as we promised ourselves to do, due to too much time spent shopping for furniture indoor and outdoor, landscaping the front and back yards and improving the interior with repair and decoration. All of a sudden, days became busier on retirement than they used to be during my working time and I began to wonder how I could make a living - had I to - on such a busy schedule! Also, suddenly, I realized that true life was not at work where things were pretty much organized, administered and directed with and by others but in an environment where your own self was the controller of the interface between your needs and desires and their realization. For years, I thought I was in charge, but now I knew that I was really in charge! Our townhouse in Jupiter rapidly became the talk of the town. We named it:"The little white house"… because it was painted white and because I was "in charge"! Nothing would have distinguished it in the block if it was not for the unique landscaping we created in the front and back of it. Anyone looking for our place could not miss it if we were only referring to it as:"The French Man tropical forest". In addition to the lush landscaping, my builder's instinct made me built a Florida room adjoining the house which was conveniently used as a dining room when no visitors were present and a bedroom when they were staying with us for a while. In order to achieve this "magic trick", all furnishing were foldable (the sofa bed, the table and the chairs except the small cloth cabinet). Needless to say that Michael was the most frequent visitor… and I built it with him in mind. We spent three years and a half in the little white house. I began to like it so much that moving away, one day, was a painful thought I preferred not to entertain. The main reason for the sentimental attachment was the friendship we developed with half a dozen of celibate women (widows or divorced) and the weekly Friday nights out we were scheduling at each other places for games drinks and snacks. From this limited friendship sprang a bigger one involving all neighbors for the annual: "block party"… However that day once came. The housing market was moving in the right direction as well as the stock market and the 401K along with it and the call for investing was too strong to resist! After considering all the alternatives we decided to go ahead; put for sale the wooded land we invested in, in Pickens county SC, with my parents inheritance, empty the 401K and the Michelin Credit Union savings account and put also for sale the little white house in order to buy the dream house on the water. The process of doing all the above began during the winter of 2012. The lots in Pickens County sold within two months in April 2013. Then we proceeded with the search for the house on the water using the web sites of Trulia and Zillow. After viewing virtually hundreds of proposals and visiting concretely a couple of dozen… we ultimately decided to land on Singer Island with a choice of one house in the southern part of the island in the town of Palm Beach Shores and two others in the northern part in the town of Riviera Beach. The house at the corner of Lake Drive and Cabana road in the Yacht Harbor Estate (YHE) subdivision wan our votes! Once our decision to go with the house in YHE was made, everything went very fast, too fast! The little white house sold in four days from posting and the closings were scheduled two weeks from the signing of the sales contract, around mid November. The Credit Union savings were transferred to my checking account in a matter of days (4 or 5 as I recall) and the 401K retirement plan was made available for a 20% reduced amount due to taxation. After meeting with my "BB&T" (my bank) investment advisor, we made few changes, such as changing the 401K into an IRA with deferred taxation and therefore were able to transfer the full amount of the plan to my checking account. Initially, I forgot about the infamous 20% which, in the end, happened to be very needed to close the sale: "cash". If it was not for that, I could not have done it cash, and should have applied for a bridge loan which would have put me in an equal footing with a competitor who was applying for a full bank loan. By paying cash I got advantage over him and could even drop the price by $10,000. All this fast and furious transactions ended two days before thanksgiving 2013 and we moved in on the eve of that holiday leaving the little white house ready to be indwelled by the new owners during the first week of December... as planned!

The house was a true paradise with its "tropical forest" encircling the swimming pool in the backyard. Actually the landscaping and the privacy it provided were the real selling points. The house itself, a vacation rental, with a three bedrooms two baths, "L" shaped, was entirely renovated, five years prior to our acquisition and was a turn-key deal requiring no further repairs or improvements before moving in. The west branch of the "L", in the front of the house on Lake Drive, was facing a wide open lawn planted with several different variety of palm trees, including a coco-tree, and dotted with travertine rocks strategically placed to prevent undesirable parking on the grass. The private driveway was partially covered by a two-car carport located across the main entrance of the house. All rooms facing the backyard had sliding glass doors which made the inside of the "L" look like a continuous glass wall connecting the interior with the exterior. In addition a back covered porch conveniently extended the indoor living quarters to outdoor living and dining spaces. We decided to name the property: "The Garden of Eden" for we never saw and sensed before a dwelling resembling so closely to what is described in the Bible. As such… it was comfortable for our bodies, relaxing for our minds, charming for our eyes and perfectly secluded to practice nudity at all times… as it was in the Garden of Eden (or, for that matter, at the cabin by the mountain lake). What a gift for naturists like us. This was our house on the water and our "oasis" on the island!

We were located less than five minutes by foot from the "Lakeworth Lagoon" on the West, a large body of water on the "Intracoastal Waterway" and no more than ten minutes to the ocean on the East. The only thing I was missing was the great aerial view of Singer Island and its vicinities as it could be seen from the top of the "Blue Heron Bridge" connecting the eastern continental side of Florida to the island. I loved to walk to the bridge and stop to ponder and meditate over the beauty of the view (which has been selected, as a background screen, by a local TV station, to report on the weather - not just by coincidence -). The bridge was my "mountain" from which I could see, at the end of the two miles long line of skyscrapers by the ocean shore on the east, the northern end of the island connecting with the "John D. MacArthur" state park; the towns of "North Palm Beach" and "Lake Park" on the North West; the "Phil Foster beach and boat park" on the West; the "Port of Palm Beach" in Riviera Beach on the South West; "Peanut Island", the towns of "West Palm Beach" and "Palm Beach" on the South; "Palm Beach Shores" and the "Palm Beach Inlet" on the South East… What a view!

THE INVISIBLE HAND

One day, as I was cleaning the gutters of the house, I stepped over the roof, and to my surprise, I could get a glimpse of the lagoon and of the Phil Foster Park at the bottom of the Blue Heron Bridge. From that moment on I kept thinking that I could bring home the great view from the bridge if only I could build a tower tall enough to look over the two story condo buildings sitting on the west side of my street. The project fully materialized when I climbed the tall ladder of a tree trimming company I hired to give a cut to the ficus enclosing my lot. Twenty four feet was all I needed to replicate the view from the bridge! If it was not for the money, I would have started right away but the money was frozen in investment contracts calling for hefty penalties for early withdrawal. My best option was to count on the cash that one day would proceed from the sale of the house in Greenville SC. That day came as my wife was preparing for one of her bi-annual trips to France to visit her mother. It was the end of April 2014. We were in Greenville, three days away from her departure when she told me that the time has come to decide whether we wanted to settle down in the Garden of Eden or else. After almost four years of commuting she reached the point of calling it quit! She wanted to grow her new roots in Florida and wished to develop as strong a network of relations as she had it in Greenville. Needless to say that I jumped on the occasion and, before we knew it, we had a realty agent from the "Merchant" realty Co. by the name of Nelly assigned to our sale. A power of attorney was established on the same day so that the sale could proceed without my wife being present... just in case, and a photographer was scheduled to come home and take pictures for the day after her departure. Here also, things moved very fast. Two days after the sale was promoted through the internet and even before a sign "for sale" was planted in the front yard, Nelly called me to announce that we had a buyer $ 8,000 short of the asked price which was in excess of half a million dollars. That was more than six times the purchase price… thirty years earlier for a house now carrying the venerable age of 103! I could not believe that the sale would come that fast and so well financially. If it was not for Nelly, who knew what she was doing, I would have never asked for the price she had posted, but I trusted her and obviously she was (almost) right on the money. On one hand, I knew that the house was sound and sturdy with a lot of potential for improvement. On the other hand I knew also that the expansion of downtown to the edge of our historic preservation area was a notable incentive, yet it was still hard to swallow how advantageous the sale was in terms of ratio of sale over purchase. I definitely believe that: "location, location, location", as "they" say, was the determining selling argument. Anyway, the sale contract was signed, thanks to the power of attorney, the following day and we all decided to set up the closing date two days after my wife's return from France, on the 29th of May 2014. The new owners, a young couple with three kids were amicable and seemed to be of a decent upbringing: him, an attorney, who redirected his carrier as a priest and her, an OBGY. He got a job as assistant priest in one of the multiple protestant churches of the area and she was assigned to the Greenville Memorial Hospital.

All of those who knew us and our house wondered how I could empty it, in three weeks - as requested by the new owner -, by myself, alone! The process began by selling some pricy pieces of furniture and artwork to friends and by keeping some others to refurnish the cabin by the mountain lake. Some more were put in storage in order to be moved to Florida. That alone took care of half of the whole furnishing of the house. The other half was taken away by a local auctioneer and sold out within a month. Actually, the fact that Chantal was away, was a blessing… in disguise for in spite of the sorrow and nostalgia of getting rid of objects very dear and familiar, I had the nerves to decide, on the spot, what was to stay and what was to go. With Chantal present I wonder if we could have parted from that much "stuff" ever!

When she returned from France, this was the first time that she did not sleep in her City bed but in her Country bed in the cabin... Not the "Little" one but the "Blue" one which Gil offered us to use, as our own, a couple of years earlier, at no other cost but maintenance. The cabin being a 24' x 24' was composed of a huge living room, dining room and kitchen, two bedrooms and a full bath. For two years, during our stays in Greenville, we turn the cabin into an intimate nest with a bedroom for Michael to use at his convenience.

CHAPTER 15

THE LAST HURDLE

The following three weeks, in the blue cabin, in the heat of the month of June, were different from any other time we have spent there before. For one, all the furniture which belonged to Gil and Sarah were removed and replaced by ours, to the delight of Amy, their daughter, who was moving to her own apartment in Clemson where she was to attend university; and for two, because the cabin became, by default, the home in SC away from home in Florida. With Michael living in Greenville, we tacitly accepted that, from now on, our lives will be spent between the Blue Ridge Mountains of upstate SC and the sandy beaches and swampy flat lands of South Florida. Respectively at the ages of sixty seven, for me, and sixty six for my wife, we were preparing ourselves for a new beginning. I was suspecting that the "invisible hand" was at work… again, but did not really know what to expect except that, for now, I will keep myself busy building the tower with all the enthusiasm of my inner youth!

Up to now our desires have been fulfilled. We were living in the tropics, on an island, by the water, in a warm climate year round, financially well off and retired. Michael was living his life independently at and with Gateway House, traveling once or twice a month, and enjoying it. His involvement and pleasure resulting from it gave us peace of mind and, all things considered, if "like father (and mother) like son" has any meaning, a sense of parenting work fairly well done...

Throughout the seemingly chaotic moves we endured when establishing ourselves as Floridians, in a relatively short period of time, I happened to experience, more than ever before and as I always thought, that the places we were at, at any given moment, were the result of a continuous process of decision making based on a binary system of "0" and "1" or "YES" and "NO" with no "backspace" or "delete" keys once the decision was made. I also convinced myself that the result of each decision was taking me one step forward or backward or sideway towards my final destination and that the steps were leaving behind the trace of a messy and tortured path of my journey through life.

I knew that from birth to death the departure and arrival points of my earthly journey were known of God because He is omniscient but always refused to consider the journey itself as being "predestined". I also kind of knew that meeting God's intended arrival point would only happen if I took His directions to finalize my decisions; otherwise, if ignoring Him and following on my own directions, I was taking a chance of getting lost and arriving at an unwanted destination. This is with this understanding that the notion of predestination defined, by some, as a preset pathway for one's life irrespective of one's free will, was bothersome to me.

The logic to oppose predestination was first, that I did not decide to reside on earth or, for that matter elsewhere in the universe at that appointed time. Second, I did not choose the process (sex and its derivatives... defined, by some, as sins) by which I was born neither my parents nor their DNA or standing in life. Third, nobody consulted with me as to whether I wanted to live and conform to a culture which was not of my making. Lastly, I realized that I had no control of the operation of the universe neither of the mental health of my mind or of the fitness of my body; needless to say that I have no control on matters of life except death by suicide. The only thing I did know was that, facing life, I was naked and afraid... This being said, I suppose that the only reasonable alternative to all of my denials and miserable conclusion would be to accept and admit that an "invisible hand" put me in this world, at this specific time, under this given set of circumstances, which are all foreign to me, and that my required contribution to that mysterious event is to submit to its will, which, for purpose of simplification, I will call: "the Will of God". The other doable option, under my control, would have been to remove myself from this unilateral deal by killing myself; a thought so unattractive that the instinct of self preservation forbid me to entertain... even for a minute! So I went on with life, not knowing how to live, refusing to die and with no understanding of the Will of God. Nobody told me what God wants from me except for the preachers of a multitude of religions (including my parents' and priest's one) who cannot agree on anything but the fact that each single one of theirs is all right while all the others are wrong, and that their teachings come from God Himself who inspired them and gave them the authority to rule, reward and punish, as necessary, for any derogation, their enslaved followers... I wanted to hear from God Himself. I wanted to hear His truth. This burning desire was the motivator which carried me from day to day, until today and hopefully beyond, since the day I heard the monk in Theix talking about Jesus.

Because of no better reason, I came to believe that God put me on earth, now, to contribute to His present metamorphosis in humans by incarnating His Spirit and expressing His Thoughts which is: "to love my neighbor as I love myself", in order for Him to establish His Kingdom on earth as it is in Heaven.

Because our distant parents: "Adam and Eve" abused and misused the gift of "happiness" given to them, in Paradise, I wanted to believe that God put me on earth to replace them and be as happy as they were so that He can continue to partake in my happiness. My decision to share my happiness with others is the way to make God partake in it! In short: just be good with others and God will have mercy on you and bring you peace! I guess that the finality of my reflection is to say that God is merciful and never abandons man but that man, in his ignorance and arrogance, does abandon God and in so doing chooses his torment. In that case, God - Omniscient - knew, from the beginning, where one's arrival point would be in spite of His help which He knew would be ignored or resisted. Although I sincerely believed that I was not predestined to fail, I was always annoyed by the idea that God did know my final destination, especially if it was bad, even before my life's journey began... Knowing that it would be bad does not mean that God wanted it to be bad because I truly believed that God has my best interest at heart and will never let me go astray without warning me or intervening directly or indirectly. In the event I missed the "gate of Heaven", I came to wonder who or what stirred me in the wrong direction. After thinking long and hard about the issue, I arrived at the conclusion that the end result is MY RESPONSIBILITY ALONE and not unchangeable genetic destiny or God's intended fatality. I also finally realized that God does let me know my upcoming destination when the relentless pursuit of happiness is rewarded with pleasure which produces constant joy and contentment… Instinctively I realized that God always speaks to man's heart by means of "intuition" and "coincidences" through people and events. In events, I figured that man determines his progress toward Heaven depending on his decisions to either fight or flee or show faith in God while confronting adverse situations. In people, I imagined that decisions partially rest in their answers to questions. Opposition or blindness to the natural inclination of the heart (and guts) to follow upon positive coincidental events or sound intuitional guidance will certainly mean moving backward but neutral impregnation by God's Holy Spirit and submission to His Will would quite surely mean moving forward… to God's delight! Wrong or right, the concept gave flesh to my quest for hearing His voice, in people, in His alleged silence and seeing His presence, in events, in His supposed absence. From that point on, I decided to relentlessly seek Him by paying a much closer attention to events and people, with mindfulness of love… at all times!

Building the tower was not as easy as I thought it would be. With my limited (and negative) experience of building a "Florida room" adjoining our town house in Jupiter Village, by myself, I decided, this time, to hire a general contractor in the hope to minimize and expedite the administrative work of the project which mainly consisted of getting a set of building plans and obtaining a construction permit. After that also, and to give me peace of mind, I wanted to rely on the general contractor to hire sub-contractors of different trades and follow-up on the construction timeline and official inspections, by the building department, until completion of the project and the delivery of the certificate of occupancy. Not knowing any general contractor, personally, I asked my friends to give me recommendations.

The first contractor who answered my call said he could not see me before a couple of weeks. I was not happy with the answer but, to please my friend, I waited till the appointed time. When this time came, he did not show up. So I called him only to hear that he has forgotten! We set another time for a week later. He showed up that time. I gave him a tour, explained my project, showed him pictures of existing towers I took in the cities nearby and handed him sketches of my vision of the shape and location of the tower with respect to the existing construction. He was attentive, listened, took notes and promised to get back in touch in the days to come. Without a sign of life for the whole following week, I decided to call him again. This time I met his answering machine which asked me to leave a message and reiterated that "my call was very important to him"! With no response two days later I left another message, sounding like an ultimatum, saying that I will call off our business relation if no answer was given within 24 hours. As expected, 24 hours later the deal was over. My friend Dale was very disappointed and so was I...

The second contractor I called was available right away. He came the following day. We went through the same procedure as with the first one. He said he will have his project manager to meet me in order to work out the technical details. Till this day I still wait for a meeting to be set! My second friend Jim, in spite of numerous calls, all answered to him with excuses, finally apologized to me for his aborted attempt...

The third contractor seemed to be the right guy for the job. He showed up with an architect he was used to work with. Both guys took the tour, saw the pictures and my sketches and took some measurements. The architect (Michael) was set by the general contractor (Gino) to begin the drawings immediately so that a "concept" set of plans could be made available for review and amendments within two weeks. I liked very much the professional approach of the team. Two weeks later the concept plans were reviewed and a set of specifications written down so that a "progress" project could be reviewed and finalized in another couple of weeks. Passed that point, with a tentative budget and, in the meantime, the completion of a survey showing setbacks and elevation, the drawing package was ready to be reviewed and sealed (stamped) by a professional engineer (P. E.) and submitted to the city's building department for the obtention of a construction permit. At this point things turned nasty. Prior to applying officially for the construction permit, I requested both, the general contractor and the architect to get together and fine tune the original budget with a margin of error not to exceed 30 %... What I received, with no reference at all to the budget established at the time of the "progress" review, was twice as much. I was mad and my friend Sandra, who recommended Gino, very disappointed!

Since, pricewise, things were not going my way, for the first time, I started to test my philosophical principle of "paying attention to events and people… at all times!" If I was true to the "event" part of the principle, I should have fled the project right away, yet something inside of me was telling me that the tower was the right thing to do at the condition to find the right "people" to do it with. Based on this assumption and the good gut feeling I had about it, I went to the internet and began to scout sites offering professional services in the home improvement fields. Finally, after a couple of hours of research, I decided to call three of the general contractors whose resumes sounded good enough to give them a shot. The first one was Dennis. Two days after meeting with him, he called off the offer pretending he was too busy to commit to a timeline. The second one Gregg, after a week or so, called proposing a price tag being twice the outrageous price of Gino and Mike! Needless to say I thanked them both without thanks! The third one, another Michael, came up with a price matching the Gino/Michael's price with a timeline of four months from the issuance of the construction permit. At that point, I came to realize, to my chagrin, that I will not be able to complete my project for a lesser price. I decided to hire him since my anger towards Gino did not abate for having missed his original estimation by 100% and misled me into a project that I might have cancelled otherwise. My stubbornness to go ahead was supported by the insisting voice of my conscience and the demand of my guts commanding me to move on. After three painful months of reviews and modifications the construction permit was granted and work began in September 2015. For the following eight months, and not four as Michael forecasted, it was like riding a rollercoaster. At times things were moving smoothly and at an even pace but at others, the unpredictable rates of speed, the turns, the unforeseen ups and downs became very taxing on my personal involvement in the project and, after a while, began to take a toll on my patience. Inspection delays, change orders, late or early deliveries, wrong materials, unavailability of contractors, conflicting schedules were my daily worries and I kept calling or texting Michael for answers that, for most of the time, he did not have. On one hand I was trying to calm my wife's impatience while Michael, on the other hand, was trying to justify the project breakdowns! Finally we made it and decided to celebrate the completion of the project on the week-end after Independence Day of 2016!

I had my tower… and now she wanted her boat! I kept delaying the purchase of the boat with a slew of good reasons. In the beginning, while living in Jupiter village, I argued that we were living to far from the water and that paying a rent for a wet slip would be unsafe and too expensive. Not to mention that the cost of maintenance of a boat seating in water, at all times, would be prohibitive or, at best, equivalent to the rent of a dock with a lift which cost wise was out of question. Keeping the boat on land, at our place of living in Jupiter, was not an option since it was forbidden by the HOA to park a boat on a trailer in the driveway or the backyard. After searching for a rental spot in the closest marinas we came to realize that what we were afraid of was true. Adding insult to injury we also discovered that rental spots were not always readily available and that, often, we had to contract the rent, in advance, and then wait for the dock to be vacated by the previous tenant at the end of his contract.

At that time these arguments were sufficient to make us wait until we find a place "on the water". When we moved closer to the water, in Singer Island, the reasons not to buy were much less obvious. There were no restrictions to park the boat on a trailer in private properties. The ramps to launch the boat were approximately three hundred yards away from my drive way, on Phil Foster Park. The only limitations were the size of the boat in order to make it fit under the covered driveway and the power of the vehicle utilized to haul the trailer and the boat. After visiting several places to buy a used boat, unsuccessfully, for different reasons, we ended up buying a brand new "15 feet Super-Sport Boston Whaler" at the "Marine Max" dealership on PGA Boulevard in Palm Beach Gardens. It happened that this boat could be hauled by my Toyota Camry, which saved me the trade and purchase of a more powerful vehicle. And besides, I hated the idea of getting rid of my car which was my faithful companion for 15 years and still running like a charm. The only thing I was uncomfortable with was my skills to back the trailer onto the ramp. I tried the maneuver many time in a deserted parking lot until I was confident enough to do it at the ramp. When "D-Day" arrived, it was a Monday when almost nobody was in the park to watch me. I backed successfully the boat to the water and freed it from the trailer... as a pro! What a relief it was! The stress faded away in no time and made me feel immediately competent in a field of activity alien to me just a while ago. The pleasure we derived from riding the ocean and the intra coastal waterway was sublime whether boating at slow speed and admiring the upper end villas by the waterway or speeding to the max on the ocean passing by the expensive condos in the high rises of Singer Island. After a couple of successful rides, we decided to go fishing in addition to boating. Success in this area was mixed but more often achieved in the waterway than at sea. We blamed it to our fishing equipment which was better designed to catch catfish, snappers, triggers, blue runners, ladyfish, needle fish, mullets, blackdrums and pompanos rather than big game king mackerels, dolphins, cobias or snooks not to mention sailfish, swordfish or other sawfish...

CHAPTER 16

ARGENTINA

Since, as retirees, we had plenty of time in our hands (and supposedly plenty of money to spend!!!) some of our older friends or others of the same age or even younger ones were talking us into cruising with them on luxury boats, around the world, from one to several weeks at a time. Although we have made this experience earlier in our lives on a cruise in the Caribbean's by the name of:"Princess", for a week, we knew what they were talking about but were not so much into replicating this kind of vacations at that time. Our preference always went to planning and organizing our vacations, mainly by ourselves, or, as needed, with some help from:"AAA" when we were, unsuccessfully, trying to access some professional websites not available to "amateurs".

We decided to go to Argentina during the month of February 2017. February is in the heart of summer in the South hemisphere and therefore a good month to visit:"Tierra del Fuego" and the:"Fin del Mundo" city of:"Ushuaia" - the farthest southern town on the planet - where temperatures vary from 5 degrees centigrade (40 degrees Fahrenheit) to 20 (68) during that period of time which is also the high season for tourism. On the other hand, as far as temperatures go, the city of: "Iguazu" - the farthest northern dwelling of Argentina - in the Amazon forest, where flow the mighty Iguazu falls, they vary from 25 degrees centigrade (76 degrees Fahrenheit) to 40 (104). In order to accommodate the variations in temperature we packed in our luggage clothes for both extremes.

Everything was ready to go when, ten days before the departure Chantal fell on the parking lot of a grocery store and broke a foot. In addition, when returning from a medical "Urgent Care" facility nearby, she broke a wrist while trying to walk on crutches provided by the doctor at Urgent Care… At that point it is needless to say that the trip to Argentina was cancelled. Fortunately, overtime, we got almost all of our money back on all reservations.

This event, which drastically affected our planning, made me think why all of that happened. My first reaction was: it is the Will of God? Why God does not want us to go there at this specific time? To that, my reaction was to think that God instigated this event to protect us from an imminent danger. Although no planes fell from the sky within the timing of our cancelled trip; neither natural nor human made catastrophes were reported in the news, I knew that, whether being addressed directly to me or indirectly through her, selectively for us only or collectively with others, that this event was the manifestation of the Divine Pedagogy at work to protect us and keep us from harm's way. The danger was never identified as such but it could have been anything from backstabbing for robbery, to being run over by a vehicle, to be arrested by error, to be injured in a street riot, to have a car accident, to… whatever that God did not want us to be in!

Believing that it was the Will of God which was at play in this situation helped to overcome the disappointment for not traveling this time, however, rescheduling was always in our mind. We did reschedule almost the same trip in November 2017 with a departure time on the 6th of February, 2018. From the beginning to the end on February 28th, everything moved seamlessly, uneventfully. It was as if the invisible hand was unrolling the scroll of our itinerary before our own eyes or unwinding a film on "3D" on the silver screen of our trip. Even the communication with the locals was easy in spite of their "Argentinean Spanish", which, depending on the regions we were in, was tinted with Portuguese, Italian, German, Dutch and numerous other colloquial languages spoken by Indians, as opposed to my "Castilian Spanish". Sometimes, for a change, we were able to speak English and even French, mainly with visitors and hotels' and restaurants' staffs. Everyone was friendly, helpful, understanding and hospitable. I always felt at home. The positive attitude of the people we met made me elaborate on the "golden rule" which says:"do onto others what you would like them do onto you" and the proverb which states:"God helps those who help themselves". For the later, after hours spent to organize the trip, I considered that God's providence was well deserved every time I was stepping outside the rental car to ask for directions, and also, when I was at a loss, that God abundantly provides for those who cannot help themselves… For the former, I realized that when somebody helps me, it is God who does it using either an angel or a saint who expresses himself through a person; but, conversely when somebody offends me, it is also God who allows it using a demon who expresses itself through a person as well. All of a sudden I discovered that planet earth was populated by live visible saints as well as by invisible virtual saints, angels and demons embodied in visible real human beings. Another concept I derived from the earlier ones was that God's providence takes over man's weaknesses and handicaps every time man asks Him to provide him His strength and wisdom to do his part of a task, no matter how small it is, in order for God to complete it... through others! The trip to Argentina confirmed to me that nobody is an island, that God is in charge and that God will always fulfill His charge.

Argentina is a big desert composed in the West by the Andes and the Sierras, in the far South, by Antartida (Antarctica), Patagonia in the middle, the Pampa and Amazonia in the north and the Atlantic Ocean on the East. In order to cover such a large amount of territory, it took a lot of travelling by airplane. Actually, all put together, it took four air round trips, three thousand miles by car and a round trip by train from start to finish. To begin with, we took the "Tri-Rail" train from Mangonia Park, nearby West Palm Beach, to the Miami airport; then an airplane from Miami to Buenos Aires; then an airplane from Buenos Aires to Ushuaia; then an airplane from Ushuaia to Calafate; then an airplane to return to Ushuaia; then another one from Ushuaia to return to Buenos Aires; then an airplane to go to the "Iguazu Falls" and another to return to Buenos Aires; then another to return to Miami and finally the Tri-Rail train to reach our final destination in Mangonia Park. Also, because Argentina is so big to visit in such a short time, it took some drastic decisions to make as to where to go and what to leave behind. The Primary four most attractive spots, emblematic of Argentina, were on our list namely: the Capital Buenos Aires, Ushuaia, the Perito Moreno glacier and the Iguazu falls. The secondary choices included: Cordoba, Mendoza and Mar del Plata. Left behind were the city of Bariloche in the Lakes district, the natural park of peninsula Valdes and the Northern old colonial town of Salta.

Buenos Aires is a multifaceted town with various barrios ranging from extremely poor in the favellas, in the outskirts of downtown, to extremely rich as in the district of La Recoletta in El Barrio Norte, San Telmo, Puerto Madero, La Boca and the government's Plaza de Mayo where is located the presidential palace - residence of President Macri, aka: "Casa Rosada", due to the pink color of its façade - and the Cathedral which was Father Bergoglio's church before he was elected Pope: "Francisco". Rio de la Plata which is the estuary of Rio Parana, flowing from the north, to the Atlantic, is also the border between Argentina and Uruguay. Actually, Montevideo the Capital of Uruguay, on the east-northern side of the estuary looks very much like the extension of Buenos Aires located on the west-southern side. What characterizes Buenos Aires is its: "9th of July Avenue" consisting of fourteen lanes, with four in the center dedicated to public transportation, and crossing through the heart of the town, over a couple of miles, and featuring in its middle an "Obelisco" similar to the monument in the Washington mall. Hotel: "Park Silver Obelisco", in which we have spent six nights at four different times, was our "base camp" connecting our north-south and east-west travels, and was located right across the Obelisco. A mythical visit to the cemetery of La Recoletta were "Evita Perone" is buried and which tomb, as expected, is the most visited one in the whole cemetery, revived images of the military repression, the rise of General Juan Perone, sold to the corrupt elite establishment to protect their wealth, his meeting with Evita, his conversion from military dictator to social justice militant under the mentorship of Evita... It was poignant to realize what love can do and that only love can make a lasting impact in the world history. Even today, Juan Perone is seen by the younger population as the hero and the savior of Argentina, not to speak of Evita who is still hailed as a Saint. The tombs are all built as mausoleums, above the ground, coffins visible through glass doors and even bones, skulls and skeleton in older dilapidated ones! All coffins in the Duarte (Eva's maiden name) mausoleum were recovered with white sheet. We did not see any of Evita's remains…

Tango, football (soccer) and an epicurean lifestyle are embedded in the Argentinean culture. We had a chance to appreciate the Tango and the lifestyle aspect of it when we attended the "Chantecler musical" at "Tango Porteno" (a restaurant-theater) where food wine and the show came together for a couple of hours of pure delight! By the way, the inhabitants of Buenos Aires do not call themselves: "Buenosarians" or something like that… but: "Portenos". Tango, once perceived as a sexually oriented degrading dance good for mariners and prostitutes, is now seen as a beacon of the Argentinean culture since it wan its "letters de noblesse" when it became "a la mode" and practiced in "guinguettes" and "cabarets" in Paris. In Argentina, Tango is danced everywhere, in plazas, terraces of restaurants and bars and even on sidewalks provided someone brings the music. For the football part of the culture, we did not attend a match but drove through the town of "Lionel Messi", the internationally known footballer from Barcelona (Spain), born and raised in: "Rosario".

Ushuaia, for any French national, is synonymous with "extreme adventure" since an environmentalist and cinematographer by the name of: "Nicolas Hulot" has named a series of documentaries he produced in the seventies and eighties: "Ushuaia". The films are as farfetched as is the town dubbed: "El Fin Del Mundo". In the beginning, "Tierra del Fuego", the island dwelling Ushuaia, was populated by Indians which were, overtime, all exterminated by the European invaders. The fires they were entertaining for survival in the Antarctic climate were the reference used to name the island. The first non-Indians settlements turned Ushuaia into a penitentiary which became a major source of revenue for those tending to the prisoners. Today, the penitentiary is a museum reflecting on that moment in history. Tourism is currently the major industry but lasts only from late December to mid-March. Cruises and tours, on land, air and by sea are the major attractions during the short summer time. When the season ends, part of the population moves back up north to keep up with their living expenses. Everything in Ushuaia is more expensive than in any other places in Argentina. Tierra Del Fuego is bordered in the north by the strait of Magellan, which allows boats to pass from the Atlantic to the Pacific oceans, avoiding the treacherous waters of the passage of Drake (between "Cape Horn" and Antarctica) and in the south by the "Beagle Canal" named after "Captain Beagle" who took "Darwin" in an expedition which was at the origin of his theory of evolution. The Beagle canal is also the border between Chile and Argentina. The trip we took, by boat, a catamaran by the name: "Rumbo Sur", took us as far south as possible towards "Cape Horn" but left us short of a couple of dozen miles from it because it is in Chilean waters. Anyway, we enjoyed the time spent at the "Pinguineria", the farthest southern Argentinean Island exclusively populated by continental penguins. We even had the privilege to spot few of the "King" ones, which usually live further south on "Tierra Antartida", and are just about twice the height of the local ones. As a side note, I would like to mention that, on our way to the Pinguineria, we saw the settlement of "Port Williams" located on the Chilean side of the Canal, much further south than Ushuaia but, according to locales, due to its small population size, does not qualify to be called "El Fin Del Mundo"… Go figure!

It is from Ushuaia that we took a plane to Calafate and then a "Remi" (The Argentinean version of "Uber") to the "Perito Moreno" Glacier, the biggest and most visited glacier of the Andes' "Parque National Los Glaciares". Lake Argentina resulting from the melting of the glacier is the biggest barren one of Patagonia.

Except for the tour boats cruising at the bottom edge of the glacier, there are no other boats on the lake, either for fishing or leisure. The glacier is three miles wide, twenty miles long and two hundred feet high. During the warmer season of summer one can hear the deafening sound of tons of ice breaking from the main body and falling to the lake...

We returned to Ushuaia from Calafate. Calafate is the name of a wild sweet dark purple berry growing on small shrubs and utilized to make jam and jelly or to perfume a local liquor and covers most of the desert land at the foothills of the southern Andes. In Ushuaia we enjoyed one more time the charm of this very colorful town (literally) and pigged out again on "parillas" of lamb from Patagonia. The next stage of our trip took us back to Buenos Aires and to the Park Silver Obelisco hotel where we were, by then, almost adopted as locales. After one more day of visit of the Capital we flew to the magic Iguazu Falls at the confluent of Argentina, Brazil and Paraguay. Our hotel: "Amerian" was anything but what we expected. It was like a fairy vision of what America could offer, as its best, in the middle of nowhere in the rain forest! Three cascading swimming pools and large beach decks were there to enjoy, surrounded with inside and outside bars and restaurants. Toucans were the attraction of the moment because it was mating season and the birds were unceasingly parading and flirting for attention from their opposite sex partners. In addition to the toucans, another unusual discovery, for us Americans, was: "Yerba Mate". Yerba Mate is an herb which is cultivated on a large scale in Argentina and is used as an infusion, cold or hot, in a special container: "la Bomba" and sucked through a pipe which allows the liquid to be absorbed leaving the grass residue in the bomba. Almost everybody around the swimming pools was sucking from a bomba. We were even offered to share a sip as a sign of hospitality and friendship. The bitter sweet taste of the liquid was surprising, at first, but became quickly familiar and welcome the second time around! For the limited time we had, we preferred to go out to town to visit around instead of lounging by the pools. Again, there was no surprise with the food which was excellent, no matter what the rating of the restaurant was, and the beer sold by the litter, always tasty and plentiful. Our visit of the Iguazu falls began by a "Remi" trip to the park and then a three kilometers ride in the jungle before debarking from a truck and climbing down a flight of stairs landing in the docks of cruising boats. Along the way we were given life jackets and waterproof pouches to preserve wallets, camera and other valuables from being drenched. Finally at boarding time we were given waterproof coveralls in order to survive the mist and splashes of water coming from the falls. The cruise lasted some forty five minutes which at time felt as "water boarding" when the boat was getting in and out from under the falls. Finally, damped but not cold, we returned to the point of departure with a feeling of awe and gratitude for having "survived" the hazards, perceived of real, of an unforgiving nature. The experience from below the falls persisted when, after a quick lunch, we took the trail that follow the falls from above. From this vantage point we could appreciate the full extent of the falls, the width and height and the noise… This one, of several natural wonders of the world, is twice as wide (1.7miles) as the Niagara falls and the height averages 230 feet. Three quarters of the falls are on the Argentinean side in the "Misiones Province" and the remaining on the Brazilian side. On the following day after the visit, we were in a plane on our way back to Buenos Aires and the Park Silver Obelisco hotel where we were welcome as family members would be!

    The following day, and a block away from the hotel, we did the paperwork to rent a car at Hertz and, in no time, were on our way out to "Cordoba", the largest town of Argentina after Buenos Aires, in the west. The five full days by car took us also to Mendoza, at the foothill of the "Aconcagua", the highest mountain of the Andes, and second to the mighty Mount Everest. In Mendoza we attended the most popular festival of the summer: "Musica y vino" (music and wine), which features the election of miss wine and graces the spectators' ears with folk's music and songs by national celebrities. It is in Mendoza that about three centuries ago, monks from Europe planted wine vines in the region and developed typical wines species such as "Malbec". Visits to winery and testing kept us busy there for a couple of days…

In between Cordoba and Mendoza we drove through the almost deserted Sierras and took a day to visit the "Quijadas" national park which, for lack of a better description, looks very much like the parks in Utha. We learned that the mausoleums, built on the side of the road, were dedicated to an Indian woman and her baby who died of thirst while trying to cross the Sierras on foot. True or false does not matter much to the believers who placed plastic bottle of water around the many mausoleums to insure that, if anyone crosses the Sierras again, he or she will find plenty of water to survive the hazardous trip.

Finally, the last leg of our land trip, from west to east, made us drive for hours on end from Mendoza to Mar del Plata, across the flat and boring "Pampa". From time to time, mainly at major road crossings, we could find a gas station and sometimes a cemetery which, we supposed, was servicing the haciendas (ranches) dispersed across the distant neighborhood. Except for the multitude of black dots (cows) covering the country on both sides of the road, the other living creatures we encountered, were gauchos (cowboys) trotting or galloping along the miles long fences preventing the cattle to cross the road. We arrived at the Atlantic beaches in early afternoon and decided to relax for a while… Although the beaches looked somewhat similar to ours in the Palm beaches in Florida, they were no match as far as the color and grain of the sand were concerned. On the other hand, although we were in the middle of the summer, the water was rather fresh and the breeze a little bit chilly. This was disappointing, but we enjoyed the sight and the rest on the beach, anyway. The return to Buenos Aires was all but easy due to the heavy traffic in the city and the lack of signalization which made us miss our point of destination at the Park Silver Obelisco hotel at least a couple of times. Once we made it at the Hertz office, it was the end of our adventure. The next day we went for a last long walk on the pedestrian "Florida" avenue and again enjoyed, for the last time, every moment of the Argentinean life.

CHAPTER 17

AT PEACE, AT LAST (PART I): FRANCE

Sipping on a "Rum and Coca-Cola", on the rocks, on the balcony of the tower, I felt as being on the top of the world and wondered, for a second, if the tower was not built just for that special moment! Enjoying a blinding fiery sunset, my thoughts flew high and beyond the clouds to look for an answer to the contentment I was experiencing. At seventy two, I was feeling satisfied, complete and full and wondering, in the state of grace I was in, if life could ever be any better and therefore whether I should put the last touch to the painting of my life, down here, before signing it good-bye! Knowing that such a decision about life and death was not of my prerogatives I kept rejoicing about an earthly life, so far, well lived...

Memories from my past were coming back to my mind. One of them was about the life and death of my beloved calf, which was slaughtered at a wheat harvest in Chateau-Gaillard. It was haunting me at times, for I felt guilty of having done nothing to prevent its killing... as if I could have! The childish but serious concern of being responsible for its death made me smile inside more than once, in my adult years but, thanks to that violent act, I cherish the event that has awaken my sensibility to "avenging" love: the kind of love which makes you forget about yourself and put your own life on the line in order to punish the molesters.

Another one was about Monique, my "bonami" from Theix. I can still picture her face framed by blond hair cut straight above the shoulders. I remember the innocent kissing, the hidings at the "four pine trees" hill, the pain I felt when she cried as I told her that my family was moving away... At that very moment, my love for her was: a "wrenching" love, the kind of love which makes you wish to be dead rather than go on living with a part of yourself missing.

While reminiscing on the past, Les Martres-de-Veyre always came first since it marked my life in more than one way. There, the priest became my spiritual father and mentor. My respect for him and obedience were total and unconditional. Thanks to him, and him probably never knowing it, I acquired the strength, courage and audacity that I was lacking until then. "Monsieur le Cure" is still living in my thoughts and, I am sure, will keep living until I die. Although, as an altar boy, I was familiar with death, or more precisely, the celebration of funerals, it is in this village that I experienced, for the first time, the death of a real person: my little sister Brigitte. It is there, for the first time also, that I felt the warmth of an entire community sympathizing with our loss.

Above and beyond all the people I remember best is: Josiane. She was the most present in my life but yet the most elusive. Josiane, whom I loved platonically - but her surely never knowing it - was my obsession. Her looks and demeanors were erotic. For me she was the impersonation of "sex appeal" at its best. She was my fantasy girl whom I could barely see or even think of without having an erection. I am sure that she was the cause of my first involuntary ejaculation and therefore became later the reason for further mental lusting and teen-age masturbation... which, of course, she never knew of! This thought, although disappointing, for a lack of personal physical engagement, was a good one, as far as nurturing sexual fantasies, and is still titillating my imagination. It was also in Les Martres-de-Veyre that we had our first television and the privacy of indoor toilets. These two items, although relatively modest by today's standards, symbolically brought the whole family from poverty to the era of prosperity and, even now, make me think how happy we all were to have access to these symbols of wealth and middle class status.

Michelin is truly the manifestation of the Invisible Hand at work in more ways than one. For one, involuntarily, it kept me from becoming a priest by providing Christian schooling (Catholic by definition) which my mother preferred over seminary. That was a good think, with regards to my love of girls and strong appetites for sexual gratification in spite of the condemnation of the Catholic Church for such sinful desires! For two, the private schooling ingrained in me the values dear to the most influential humanistic lay philosophers of our ancient and modern times along with the Catholic Church teachings... which, to a certain extent, reconciled me with the idea of being a Christian outlaw, or heretic, for not heeding the call for priesthood, but yet making me a respectable individual by all the lay thinkers' standards.

The cowboy's cartoons were also things that I enjoyed a lot! For me, beyond the stories themselves, they were the materialization of concepts of power, fair play, honesty, truthfulness, loyalty, passion and compassion; dreams where the good guys were always winning and bad guys always loosing. Needless to say that in our games of war, each clan looked at itself as the "good guys". On both sides, losses were always justified as wins in order to motivate the troupes for the next fight. I considered the morals of the cartoons as powerful, if no more, than the teachings of the Catholic catechism in churches or the tenets of lay civic and civil instruction in schools... But my mother was very displeased to see me, at the age of fourteen, still indulging in these childish readings. One day she decided to forbid me buying this kind of junk anymore (by cutting my allowance) and also threatened me to burn all the books I kept lined-up on the shelves of my bookcase. To save her the effort I burnt the books myself. During the whole process I remember rationalizing my decision by telling and repeating to myself that she was right and that I needed to grow in wisdom beyond cartoonists' philosophy! This destructive performance raised in me the sentiment that even the most cherished things in life do not deserve idolatrous worship.

It was in les Martres-de-Veyre also that I realized I was not French! For me, French meant that I was a member of a community which spoke my language and adhered to the ways of life that the priest preached in the church, the teacher taught in school and the mayor protected with the full enforcement of the law of the land. And actually, in this aspect, my family and I were certainly more French than any French could be as far as adhering and respecting the French ways of life and obeying the law of the land! I was disappointed but thanks to that disappointment I decided to behave in a way that will definitively define me and my family as fully acknowledged, assimilated and adopted French citizens of les Martres-de-Veyre. Through the church as an altar boy, school as the first of the class, my involvement in the municipal marching band and the local soccer team... it worked! Thanks to the positive attitude of most of the villagers I will always call les Martres-de-Veyre:

my Hometown. Thus, it was in les Martres-de-Veyre that I became officially French through naturalization. Although it did not make any difference between the "before" naturalization and "after", as far as daily life was concerned, I knew then and secretly enjoyed the pleasure of belonging to a nation. I was no more the "apatride", the man without a country, I was French! I remember that it showed on the day we crossed the Italian border to visit Turin and its shroud. The priest handed to the border custom officer twenty two ID French national cards along with his passport and the driver's. This time my papers were no different from these of the other boys, as I recall it was the case a couple of years earlier, when we crossed the border with Switzerland. At that moment, at the Italian border, I felt as if the whole world was acknowledging me as a Frenchman.

The shroud of Turin was the strongest revelation I have ever had about my Hero: Jesus Christ. It was much more powerful than His teachings or whatever the church was telling about Him. It was Him in person! As such, I could relate to Him as my Master, my Teacher, my Friend and even my Brother. Why, Him the Son of God, and me, a Child of God, could not be related as brothers? This concept of brotherhood is still very alive in me today and I thank the priest for that... as I thank him for having "contaminated" me with the virus of traveling, which, even very recently, took my wife and I to Argentina! As far as traveling goes, the souvenir of my "Citroen Traction 11 BL" and the family vacations we took on the resorts of the Atlantic Ocean, until the poor thing died on a road to the monastery of: Abbey de Sept Fonts, for a lack of motor oil, continues to make me sick in my stomach. We owned a car which was the ultimate achievement of the middle class status. And of the whole family, I was the sole driver of the machine! Killing the car, by pure negligence, still haunt me as if it was yesterday. Its replacement by an Opel Record (GM) helped to heal the pain of the loss but could not erase my love for the Citroen from my memory. That event taught me the lesson to never procrastinate any maintenance of things (and people alike), no matter how insignificant it seems, in order to avoid the self inflicted pain it triggered. It is also a reminder that I was the family's chauffeur. Something that my wife had a tough time to cope with, but ultimately recognized as being the most sacrificial present I could have offered to parents unable (my father) or intimidated (my mother) to obtain a driver's license.

Similarly to the "travel drive" virus from the priest, another one was the "photography drive" virus inoculated by my physics and chemistry professor at college: CHARRAS. This hobby was my passion as tons of picture albums, slide boxes, super 8 movie reels, video tapes and DVD discs can witness on my behalf! Travel, photography and its derivatives: slides and movies shows have occupied most of my leisure life until now where, at any opportune occasion, I rush to my camera for a shot. Another "drive" a.k.a. "sexual drive" overwhelmed me when the chemistry of my maturing body established a direct connection between my brain and my genitals… and, at times, flooded my imagination with lustful thoughts inducing, on occasion, obsessive compulsive masturbation. It is in les Martres-de-Veyre that the game of chasing girls began, as a second nature, and continued on, in Clermont-Ferrand, becoming more and more sophisticated with time and practice.

Leaving Les Martres-de-Veyre was painful because it was like dying to my youth and to all that was involved with it: the familiar countryside, the lifetime friends (supposedly but not really), the burgeoning social life, the first rush of testosterone, the first car, the family mausoleum in the cemetery which could be reached, from home, in ten minutes, by foot… On the other hand, living in Clermont-Ferrand was joyful because it was like being born again to a new mature life which brought with it: Anne-Marie and the hope she would fall in love with me; the military service and the thrill of becoming a paratrooper and a drill-sergeant; the first professional assignment at Michelin as a technical teacher for employees' continuous improvement; the brotherhood of my two best friends: Tony and Cab… but also the treason of my best friends, who married before me and the loss of Anne-Marie's friendship who married Yves (the guy with the "Gordini" sport's car)!

Never the less living in Clermont brought the biggest blessing of my life: the girl who became my wife! Thanks to her, the "white knight" in me had a chance to show off. Her kidnapping from the claws of her tyrannical father was the first, and still is, the best accomplishment of my lifetime. We married in Clermont-Ferrand with her repentant father leading her to the altar which, in itself, was the second best of my accomplishments, as far as forgiving him and keeping the two families united!

The honeymoon trip and the itinerary which took us to: Saint Tropez and more precisely to the beach of: Pampelone became, involuntarily, the discovery road of Naturism which we then worshipped for years in: Ile du Levant and elsewhere, as a philosophy, and practiced as a lifestyle. It originated in: Residence Helios and continued in: Heliopolis where it fully matured… but also gave birth to "Eroticism". I wondered if our sex life and fidelity to one another would have ever been so transparent, faithful, fruitful and complete if it was not for taking the "~~wrong~~ right turn" which, on the third leg of our honeymoon trip, landed us on the beach of Pampelone…

It is in Clermont-Ferrand that our son Michael was born as a miracle kid in the midst of multiple miscarriages. When Chantal was rescued from her miserable life at her parent's house and lived at my parents' home, she confessed, when my sister was pregnant, that she had no periods - except on rare occasions - and wondered if she could ever have a baby. I took her concern into my own hands and began a thorough follow-up on her condition with a gynecologist, who as an older dad, with both of us, explained that Chantal's condition was not hopeless but certainly aggravated for not having been treated earlier during her adolescence. Anyway, Michael was born and even if I see my contribution as "minimal", it is my third and greatest accomplishment.

It is in Clermont-Ferrand that Chantal achieved her dream of becoming an artist. It is in Clermont-Ferrand that I had a taste of politics. It is from Clermont-Ferrand that, for six years in a row, I traveled and labored almost every week-end, to bring Enval to the point of completion by either performing some tasks by myself or supervising the construction site with my friends: "Jean-Claude" the architect and another: "Jean-Claude" the "Credit Agricole" banker at the local branch of Vic-le-Comte. Both made my fourth memorable accomplishment come true. Enval must have had a very special charismatic character since it was pictured in the magazine: "l'habitat en Auvergne", with the title:" une maison qui a une ame" (a house with a soul).

CHAPTER 18

AT PEACE, AT LAST (PART II): AMERICA

A thinker once said that: "leaving is dying a little"... Actually, for having lived it through, I would say that leaving is definitively dying to one's past. By accepting the "1977 assignment" in the USA, I involuntarily decided to put an end to all the aspects of my life, as I knew it in France, in spite of my claims, to whoever wanted to listen to me, that it was temporary. And it could have been that way if the Invisible Hand had not decided otherwise! Otherwise, why was I offered to go to Egypt upon my return from the US? Why was I offered to return to the US when the Egyptian project collapsed? Why was I offered to remain in Greenville when the Texan project failed? Why? Some nice people would say that I have demonstrated the resilience and the skills required to work abroad with foreigners; some not so nice people would say that I was granted what I begged for… which was my wish to "immigrate" to the US at the expense of the Company… as if it was, for it, a normal business practice! And why, finally, when my assignment as a recruiter and trainer ended, was I offered the job of head of an engineering design department for the entire operations in North America? As far as I am concerned, the Invisible Hand was the only one to be thanked… or blamed for! Deep inside there was no doubt that only gratitude and thanksgiving were worth considering in this case.

One thing for sure, that our decision to live in the USA did, was to end most, if not all, of our friends' and family's relationships. For some it was jealousy for being blessed with opportunities alien to them; for others it was simply a natural break down due to separation by distance. Needless to say that our sexual games consisting of swinging and consensual cheating did not resist the test of time either but did not raise any desire for it anymore. To date, only a handful of family members and friends are still corresponding with us and are sometimes visiting us in the US. Again, the decision to leave France helped to weed out the chaff from the grain. And, in spite of the losses, that was good too!

Another good thing was to discover the American "Deep South". Nothing has prepared us for that. The discovery led us to never believe what is said or written about a country and its people before one experiences it… For us the American experience was outstanding in two ways: the first was about the dichotomy between the North and the South in terms of heritage, culture and lifestyle; and the second, about the "hypocritical gap" between Southern individuals' public and private lives… "Everybody's nice", "you're a good boy", "bless her heart" and "do what I say, not what I do", etc… were some of the common idiotic sayings but yet major obstacles I had to overcome, in society and at work, in order to fit in. That also, in terms of adaptation, helped me greatly to understand my mellow fellow (Rebels) Southern Americans so different from the rude direct (Yankees) Northern Americans so much closer to the European culture.

The final move to the USA, in July 1983, was filled with a lot of expectations and a little bit of sorrow. The house in Enval was put for rent for the first time... and that saddened my heart, although it was rented at first to in-laws. On the other side of the Atlantic, it was replaced, and kept me busy renovating, by a "Dutch Colonial" mansion which, by design, was the opposite of our French "troglodyte" dwelling. One was rustic, rough and country, the other was sophisticated, cozy and city! Michael did not regret a bit his time at the boarding school and was looking forward to go to an American school (he hated the discipline of the French school in Greenville!). As for Chantal she was impatient to start all over again practicing art but this time in "metal sculpting"! For me, I was nervous and exited to get in the thick of my new job and prove to myself and others that the Company's confidence in me was not in vain...

Naturism, which we have practiced for years in France, was obviously inviting itself in the USA as well. We did our homework well and found out, to our chagrin, that the "Puritan South" was not rich in places favoring this lifestyle! Only two places, at a distance of about one hour and a half, were available and nothing closer... until we received the unbelievable phone call from "Jack"! His proposal to work with him in establishing a naturist club in his breathtaking property, at the foothills of the Blue Ridge, by a man-made lake, was short lived... Nevertheless, the outcome of this memorable adventure, gave us the opportunity to enjoy, until now, the privilege of sharing the property with Sarah.

Thanks to Gil (now dead) and Sarah, the Little Cabin became sacred because of all the tribulations it has witnessed in our American life. It saw our struggle to adapt and adjust to a culture impregnated with bigotry and hypocrisy, it saw our reconciliation after a breakdown caused by too many unnecessary social and professional commitments, it saw our "renaissance" to love and life thanks to the book on Meditations, it saw our recognition of God's blessings in our life as never before... On a personal note, it saw me looking for God and finally Him finding me! Alleluia!

Thanks to Gil and Sarah, the Blue Cabin became our home away from home! Refurnished with some of our own furnishings from Greenville it gave us a sense of continuity for our uninterrupted and lengthy presence in South Carolina. This is where we were now inviting our friends living in South Carolina to wine and dine and, for some of them, the discovery of that wonderful place, in the middle of nowhere, for the first time, make them say they preferred the cabin than the house in downtown! It might be true… but I suspect that the comments were also to encourage Chantal to enjoy the simplicity of the cabin while still mourning the majestic interior Victorian decoration of the house in Greenville that she created, and was so proud of.

Chantal's dream to become a metal sculptor never truly materialized and finally died with the death of Clyde (to whom I hold no grudge). Her modeling episode was interrupted by bulimia and the subsequent three months detoxification from diet pills. Her volunteering, as an art teacher, at the youth correctional detention center in Simpsonville, in the outskirt of Greenville, was ended when the center was closed for lack of funding and her teaching experience, as a substitute French teacher was upended when she questioned some disrupting students, at: "Greenville High", if they were mentally retarded… In other words she was fired by a school system which was considering "healthy" confrontation of bad "apples" as an insult to human rights and a threat to their careers! All of these events made her more mature and, slowly but surely, she became less exalted by her entourage and more in control of her frustration. Figuratively speaking, she returned to a home she had deserted for alluring mirages. Her new hobbies were cooking, painting, Golf Croquet at NCC (the National Croquet Club in West Palm Beach) - as a substitute to golf due to back problems - and Mahjong. She is joining her groups of players on Tuesdays and Thursdays leaving us plenty of time for boating and fishing on Mondays and for me scuba diving about two times a month on days of morning high tide at the Blue Heron Bridge, playing billiard with my buddies on Wednesday nights and going to the gym on Tuesdays and Fridays.

Every other quarters Michael comes to visit us in Florida for approximately two or three weeks at a time and we spend time with him at the cabin, every other quarters, following his visits. May and October are our months of choice whereas July and December/January are his (for the Holidays)… with flexibility on both sides.

Before I retired, Michael was my biggest nightmare as far as finding a satisfactory solution for our separation. We discussed his visits to Florida and our stays at the cabin in South Carolina, yet it was not sufficient. I was looking for a way to stay in touch (almost physically) to insure that he feels our continuous presence in his vulnerable life due to his fragile mental condition. The telephone was the solution. We promised each others to call every single day to say Hello and share the events of the day. Although boring as it may seem, the solution worked beautifully! Actually it gave Michael a greater sense of independence while relying on us for any problem he might encounter at any time, day and night! I also swore to him that in case of an emergency, I would be just ten hours away from being on his side. As I write these lines, eight years into my retirement, Michael grew in wisdom to a point where he is more concerned about our wellbeing than he is by his. He is the one who now say: "do what is best for you" and: "what can I do for you to help you (in your isolation) in Florida, away from me and your friends in Greenville"? The telephone was already our physical means of communication and our training opportunity while we were still commuting every three months between the Little White House in Jupiter and the house in Greenville. At that time and in addition to calling every day, Michael played the role of the "mailman" once a week on Wednesdays. Since we kept our mailing address in Greenville, he was visiting the house, which he had the keys of, and sorted the mail, with me on the phone, to retain only the useful mail from the junk mail. Having the keys of the house gave him also the opportunity to spent time in the house, by himself, every time, as once he confided to me, he had the blues… After sorting the mail and trashing the junk he was going to the main post office, on Washington Street, at a fifteen minutes walking distance, to weigh and mail a large craft envelope of weekly correspondence. This routine ended when we established our residency on Singer Island in Riviera Beach, Florida, on Thanksgiving's Day of 2013.

Now that the house has been sold and renovated it does not represent anymore what was our home, yet Michael continues to walk by and say hello to the new owners who, overtime, acquainted with him and since then always greet him as a friend. In this house Michael became the American "Frenchy" as he was called in school. In this house he was relaxing when returning from camping as a boy scout. In this house he partied at his sacrament of confirmation as well as his graduation from High School and celebration of his Navy Junior ROTC training completion. From this house he commuted from week-ends at home to college in Spartanburg. In this house he found refuge when the "bug" of mental illness bit him… unexpectedly. In this house he found the strength to apply for work when he realized that his studies were interrupted forever. From this house I saw him going to work to "McDonald" and "Little Caesar's" and many other menial jobs placement as if no more gratifying future was in the horizon… It was in this house that we met Phil and Nancy, the directors of Gateway House who saved Michael from despair by giving him hope in him and his future! This house must have had also a special charisma for, besides having witnessed the events just described, it has been featured twice in local newspapers and magazines!

From this house we flew to France for the burials of my father in 1989, of my mother in 2005, of my father in law in 2011 and of my mother in law in 2015.

When I think of my father, I feel pity for him. The "poor devil" was never given an opportunity to amount to anything. He never went to school, never had a chance to socialize except in the very limited space of the farm he grew up in and the similarly uneducated people around him. When the Nazis took him away from home, it was the first and last long distance trip he has ever taken in his life… for worse or better, we will never know! Now I understand why he drowned himself in booze to forget the misery of a meaningless life where he could not communicate fluently in any of the languages of the countries he was deported to. His wife, my mother, was the only person he could confide in (in Polish) but, I guess, his drunkenness barred them from any genuine intimate conversations other than making scenes and insulting each others. I and my sister could have been substitutes to my mother's defection, but the lack of understanding of his condition made us more critical of him, as a delinquent father, than the object of our affection. I tried, as a young adult, to come close to him. I took him fishing. I convinced my mother to spend Sundays at a country restaurant with dining and dancing with a live band. During our summer vacations, on the ocean, I forced him to play beach volley… None of that really worked. While fishing, he was more often downing a glass of wine than pulling a fish from the water. At the restaurant, too much before lunch drinks made him almost crippled to dancing. Needless to say that beach volley made him so thirsty that he could not finish lunch before falling asleep for the rest of the afternoon! For everybody it was too much to handle. We all gave up on trying to make him happy and decided, instead, to be respectful and polite, especially during the last years of his life when he was bedridden most of the time. I believe that being incapacitated physically and mentally largely contributed to an early death since his life, prior to the accident was essentially: WORK, WORK and WORK. I wish his life, although wasted partly due to boozing, was not completely lost. As for us, his death removed the burden of hopelessness, as counselors, and the one of helplessness as caretakers. I wish him rest in peace!

My mother who also happen to be the wife of my father, is still a mystery as to why she married him, however, for me, she is a personality much easier to apprehend for I identify to her much more than to my father. Resilience, ambition, courage, sacrifice, sense of duty, patience, perseverance and stubbornness are the virtues and vices we share. She was always clear about what she wanted for us all, as a family, and as members of a foreign community. She wanted the kids (especially me) to be successful in life as far as making a living and perfectly integrated as French citizens. She pushed my father to his limits as far as putting food on the table but failed to teach him French or make a gentleman of him! I assume she loved him… but it did not show. After WWII, by refusing to return to Poland, I suppose that, at times, she felt guilty and ashamed for having uprooted him from his native country without too much for him to say… but I am not sure. What I do know, for sure, is that she was entirely devoted to the welfare and protection of her family. On one hand, her death, which ended a life of service, is her victory and a motivation for us, as her grateful beneficiaries. On the other hand, her death, which also ended a life of sacrifice, is her honor and an encouragement for us, as her respectful survivors who always counted on her. I wish her rest in peace!

My father in law was very ambitious but recognized that him and schooling did not mix well. To compensate for a lack of higher education, he developed a sense of pride in whatever he was good at and, accordingly, adopted an attitude that suited his perceived successes. All of that was to project a sense of unquestionable dignity and righteousness which would give him authority over his family, derive respect from his peers and draw compliments from his superiors. Since he was very subservient to the notions of hierarchy and chain of command, he could not tolerate any opposition to his decisions from subordinates (including, and above all, his family). In one word or in thousands, he was behaving as a submissive subject kissing up to his superiors (of whom I was part of - and easy to figure out why -), as a self declared enlightened dictator with his peers and an indispensable benevolent tyrant with his family and subordinates. He believed that all what he was doing was just and good, for the betterment of everybody by means of wrath and punishment. What a character! Anyway, his death put an end to his obsessive compulsive control of others. His death also freed his enslaved dependents and, if nothing more, gave whoever knew him, an extreme definition of arrogance! I wish him rest in peace!

As for my mother in law, she was the innocent victim of her tyrant husband. She surrendered her life to his authority without questioning. Since she was born and grew up in a culturally dominant Arabic/Muslin environment, she submitted to the rules of the land, as far as behaving in public, and continued to do the same when they moved to France. No, she did not have to wear a veil or walk five steps behind her husband when she was going outside, but the morale restrictions of the "modesty" dress code imposed by her husband were more stringent than being imprisoned in a full blown "burka". At home, she was the slave she was supposed to be by virtue of her sex… I loved her very much and she loved me! I was the first male who respected her as a female and a human being. What a change for her since even the male friends or family members of her husband were not allowed to engage with women for a real conversation except for exchanging greetings and banalities and, eventually, were reprimanded if they went beyond that! Men with men and women with women, was the rule. I am so happy that she finally decided to no longer surrender to her husband's will when I kidnapped her daughter. So, she tried her best but, at times, she had to let go for the sake of her husband's pride or simply because she was tired of fighting. Nevertheless she kept trying and I admired her for that. I was her hero and I must admit that my wife (a little) but mainly her sister despised me for it! Her death is a testimony to: relevance. I have no doubt that God will recognize her as the innocent victim who tried to affirm herself as a person and His child. I wish her rest in peace!

CHAPTER 19

THE MYSTERY OF FAITH

The sunset fiery sky is now giving way to a grayish cloudy night. There is nothing left in my empty glass. The timer has turned the lights on, inside and outside the tower, automatically. Since, I, myself, have programmed the timer, I know, without a shadow of a doubt that it must be eight o'clock at night! By looking at my glass, my mind, prompted to get more of the missing cocktail, sets up momentarily on the concepts of nothingness and emptiness...

The first wandering thought was: what if nothingness was the ultimate and true meaning of death? What if death was nothingness? Well, if it is, so be it! After all if nothing is felt after death it might be much better than the endless tremendous sorrow and torment in "hell" guaranteed for the "bad people"… but eventually not so much worse than the endless immeasurable rejoicing in "heaven" for the "good ones", as promised in the Christian scriptures? Some people say that nobody goes to hell for hell does not exist and is just a fabrication to scare the hell out of bad people and similarly heaven is also a fabrication for the opposite reason! So, if the definition of nothingness, at death, is not linked to the notions of good and bad what difference does it make if, during her lifetime, a person is or does good or bad? And why, instinctively and unconsciously, are the notions of good and bad ruling one's life from birth to death? And why man discovered these notions when he became conscious? Conscience, a thing that no living creature can share with man! And finally, why the perceived bad people should undergo martyrdom during their lives and ultimately go to hell, at death, because of their own singular definition of: "good" while others are granted good lives and, at death, eternal rest in peace, without questions, because of their adherence to philosophies and ideologies which rule their own limited world?

Reward and punishment is the answer!

Usually people (believers and unbelievers alike) do "good" to avoid punishment or obtain a reward, and depending on where you live, at what given time and which people you associate with, are the ultimate motivators to behave one way or the other and perform accordingly. What is seen as "bad" by some people at some points in times and places can be considered as "good" by others at the same or other times in the same or other places. Conscience is trained from birth to death to acknowledge and support these "local" motivators and is rewarded or punished in order to stay in line… In other words, across time and space, man's moral values depend on how he perceives himself in his current environment! For the rulers, either in the name of the People or in the name of God, or both, the objective is to: "moralize" their enslaved subjects. Morality is the means to define and codify individual and social behaviors which end result is to obey the laws in order to safeguard public order and enforce the power of the rulers! For that end, rulers invent rules, turn rules into laws, often write their own "holy book" - as in religions or lay constitutions - teach without compromise, are inflexible, exclude others, coerce others, set unachievable standards and reward hypocrisy. Under these circumstances, man's choice is either to submit to the law, no matter whether he likes it or not, stay quiet but always afraid of being inappropriate… or face lawlessness and the fear of being caught by law enforcement appointees, unless he hears the voice which breaks all the rules and laws established by men. The voice of Jesus! The voice of the one who did not fear being brought into human life by a single mother, who did not fear being raised in a human family by a foster father, who did not fear growing up in a poor and humble environment, who did not fear to work as a menial manual worker, who did not fear to associate with human "trash", who did not fear to pay attention to "low" lives, who did not fear to acquaint with prostitutes, who did not fear to point out goodness in alleged criminals and thieves, who did not fear to condemn popular righteousness, who did not fear standing for political incorrectness… the voice of the Christ who did not fear to be right or wrong or good or bad; the voice of the Christ who brought: LOVE as the ultimate non-violent weapon to fight and defeat evil and CHARISMA to achieve success with grace! The "political" message of Christ is: seek the truth, fear not, judge not, have pity and love one another.

If defeating evil is Christ's objective, why Christians should not be equipped, as He was, with the audacity to "show the other cheek"? Why Christians would not be empowered, as He was, with the assurance of victory against all oppressions? And if Christians are equipped and empowered, why should they be afraid? That is why Pope John Paul the second opened his inaugural speech with the phrase: "do not be afraid". Do not be afraid because death is not nothingness. Because death is the rebirth to a new life as Christ has demonstrated physically with His own death and resurrection. Without this powerful demonstration the message of Christ would have been vain and to no avail. But it was not in vain as one should remember the martyrdom of the early Christians who drew from Him the courage to love till the end… And also the dedication of all the people of "good will" who promote "altruism" and exercise "charity" as the practical application of the sentiments of "love" according to the teachings of Christ…

So if death is not nothingness, what about emptiness? What if emptiness was the ultimate and true meaning of life? What if life was emptiness? Well, if it is, so be it! And many people live their lives as if it was so! As the "Dalai-Lama" once said: "people live like they will never die and die as if they have never lived"! What a very forceful definition of emptiness. Contrary to animals, which I see as creatures complying to the Dalai-Lama's statement on life, men are "human living" and also "human doing" creatures. By design (in the image of God), man is meant "to live" and "to make a living". If on one hand: living should focus on loving, as exemplified by "Mary" the sister of "Lazarus" (who Jesus resurrected), on the other hand: doing does focus on making a living, as demonstrated by "Martha" the other sister of the same Lazarus. Guess which one Jesus said had the best part? Mary! And guess which part is embraced by most humans? Martha's!

Having been already nine years in retirement, I understand what making a living means, but now, more than ever, I also understand that happiness is: loving what you do and doing what you love, without prejudice, for prejudice generates undue preoccupations. As Saint Paul said: "be always occupied but never preoccupied"… For preoccupations take you to a world of negative thinking and emotions which, if not eliminated promptly, would, without doubt, interfere with and destroy the love required to complete any tasks at hand!

According to the scriptures, disobedient Adam was condemned to: "eat his bread (make a living) by the sweat of his brow" and Eve to "give birth in pain" also defined as labor or travail (travail means: work, in French). Such a reading of the scriptures gives an image of work as negative as it could possibly be. As if God wanted His humanity to spend their lives in "forced labor camps" and suffer needlessly and endlessly, simply because His "Godly Children" dared to try something (eat the fruit) He told them not to eat! What kind of omnipotent and loving God is that? What kind of selfish God, or for that matter: father, could do that? None, of course, which demands a further explanation of what the scripture calls the "Goodness of the Lord"…

Here again, the notions of reward and punishment come into play!

Since God gave dominion over the Garden of Eden to Adam and Eve, His intention was for them to cultivate and enjoy His creation. In one word: be happy. God's intention was also for them to learn "Science" by discovering the laws of "Nature" which govern His creation… For ignorance is the surest way to end up in devastation! Yet, Adam and Eve, preoccupied by learning through trying and testing (and tasting) everything in the Garden, decided to take a shortcut, assuming that eating the "forbidden fruit" will give them instant knowledge of good and evil, and by so doing would save them time and effort in their immature (they were children after all) search of quick answers as to what was good and what was bad! Unfortunately, what eating the forbidden fruit taught them was that there are no shortcuts to good responses and that only time and effort spent in observing, in studying, in comparing, in experimenting and in reproducing would end up as such! On the other hand, eating the forbidden fruit might have also alluded to the fact that predatory behavior and wreckless abuse of the Gardens' goods could be an acceptable alternative to God's intention for them to cultivate His creation! To not eat the forbidden fruit was the pretext to awake Adam's conscience, by forcing him to make a choice (obey or disobey), but also to clearly define work - cultivation - as "the law of goodness" (honesty, integrity and truth) and laziness - predation - as "the law of evil" (deceit, corruption and extortion). Viewed from this angle, one can see that good work is rewarded with the fullness of God's support who could have said Himself: "no pain no gain" and: "who works in his garden works hand in hand with Him", whereas bad work or a lack of is punished with His mighty wrath…

From my point of view, nothingness at death and emptiness in life are concepts that make sense only to those who see themselves as: "nothing and empty". To those who believe in "chance" and "luck". To those whose chance is the name of God and luck is the name of Miracle. To those whose chance and luck is the "visible heaven"… of the blinds! Their only hope is either to believe that eating, drinking, fornicating, etc… and being merry is the ultimate objective in life or, at a slightly higher level that they have contributed to make life on earth, in general: better! Always better, why not indifferent or even worse? After twenty thousand years in the making and in spite of having brought forth electricity, automation, wireless communications, computers, robots, artificial intelligence, scientific medical and healthcare advances, industrial ways of global nutrition and motorized means of locomotion, nobody can seriously say that it has made life: better (better defined as a progress towards universal peace and the global fraternal application of the golden rule). If technology has definitively made life easier why has it not contributed to make life better? My simple take on that is that "easy" rhymes with "lazy" and that lazier we become and more prone we are to become predators than cultivators of the Garden of Eden! Predators covet, steal, abuse and misuse the wealth embedded in Nature by God or entrusted by the same God in those who honestly won it and responsibly share it. Predators, by dishonestly acquiring and greedily withholding God's wealth from others become the physical manifestation of Evil on earth. Simply stated, cultivators are altruistic beings and predators egotistic ones. When wrongly exploited, to the point of annihilation, some say that Nature will take care of itself, "leak its wounds" and regenerate itself, which seems to be true, overtime, except that Nature does not do anything by itself other than "manifesting the Doer" Who invisibly works on it! And what about Science, which by the account of some, should solve all earthly problems and, ultimately, make us as wise if not wiser than God (remember Adam)? Here also, we have to remember that science does not do anything by itself other than "codifying the laws of Nature". Science does not create laws but merely discovers them and turn them into practical applications. There are surely more laws to discover and more applications to derive from them, but no matter how far and how long we go and how high or deep, our knowledge will always be dependent upon God's creation...

I was always amused by the interest and money spent in finding life elsewhere other than planet earth. In my opinion, such a discovery would be the victory of those who claim that God does not exist since, by definition, God is: "Life in a Body (Man) and in Nature, on Planet Earth". Only when life is discovered elsewhere in the universe, other than earth, will I redirect my allegiance to God... as I know it - as did some scientists and philosophers after realizing that earth was not flat -! Until that time comes, I will always consider life as the privileged attribute of planet Earth and

Earth as the unique relative centre of a complex multi-dimensional coordinates system which locate precisely humanity and life in the universe. In this system, size wise, I see man, by God design, as being midway between the worlds of the infinitely large and the infinitely small so that both worlds become accessible to his scientific discoveries… In other words, I want to believe that God has chosen Earth as the center of the celestial infrastructure which supports life and has created Man as His "Avatar", with Jesus for "model" and Adam as a "prototype", in order to complete His creation through Man's psychosomatic evolution… and work!

The timer has turned the lights off, inside and outside the tower, automatically. Since, I, myself, have programmed the timer, I know, without a shadow of a doubt that it must be ten o'clock at night! The simple programming of the timer, which gives me the knowledge of time without checking my watch, reminds me again of a cynical and skeptical French philosopher and "seeker" of God by the name of: Voltaire who, on his deathbed cried: "more I think and less I can think that this clock works and has no clockmaker"! Along with Voltaire, thinking about my own life, I want to cry: "more I think and less I can think that I live and have no life giver"!

From Germany to France to the United State of America; from Haltern to Orleat to Theix to les Martres-de-Veyre to Clermont-Ferrand; from Greenville in South Carolina to Riviera Beach in Florida; from rising from poverty to upper middle class; from living in almost slum like, unsanitary habitats to nearly high end outstanding dwellings; from being an apatride to becoming a French citizen and then an American one while keeping a dual citizenship; from being a bachelor to becoming a husband and a father; from overcoming the egotistic addiction to sexual gratification to embracing altruistic lovemaking, I can see the Divine "pedagogy" of the invisible hand of God at work, in my own life, everywhere and at all times! A pedagogy which has neither rewarded nor punished me into an enslaved position; a pedagogy which is formation of thinking; a pedagogy which formation of thinking causes evolution and elevation of thinking; a pedagogy which led us to rejoice in naturism and enjoy eroticism; a pedagogy which steady hand has always held me and guided me through good times and bad times; which has never let me depart from the God given gift of honesty and the paramount sense of duty; which has backed me up in my fights against the forces of envy, jealousy, greed, mockery and vengeance with integrity, fairness and firmness; which has granted me in abundance the pleasures of good desires, as it pleased It, and protected me from the bad desires which would have offended It; which gave me the serenity to undergo and assume fully my sexuality either in conventional or unhinged enjoyment or in ascetic voluntary abstinence or in unwanted impotence; which made me accept all unforeseeable maladies and infirmities, physical and mental as a warning or a cure for my uncontrolled excesses. The invisible hand has always been and will always be in charge! It has and will always hold my hand… What a good feeling it is to know that I was never alone in my journey from God, at birth, to God, at death, the day I deliberately decided to partake in the mystery of faith!

Another book by Bogdan J. Wnuk

(…and the data base for the current one)

Meditation on the Divine Legitimacy of man

By

The bet of divinity

The reflex of kindness

For

The salvational revolution

Library of Congress Control Number: 2009904877

ISBN:

Hardcover, 978-1-4415-3765-2

Softcover, 978-1-4415-3764-5

Ebook, 978-1-4415-7682-8

Published by Xlibris

www.ingramcontent.com/pod-product-compliance
Lightning Source LLC
LaVergne TN
LVHW011826060526
838200LV00053B/3918